Awaken the Wonder

Laying the Foundation

BRENDA HICKS

WestBow
PRESS®
A DIVISION OF THOMAS NELSON
& ZONDERVAN

WestBow Press books may be ordered through booksellers or by contacting:

WestBow Press
A Division of Thomas Nelson & Zondervan
1663 Liberty Drive
Bloomington, IN 47403
www.westbowpress.com
1 (866) 928-1240

ISBN: 978-1-9736-0130-2 (sc)
ISBN: 978-1-9736-0131-9 (e)

Library of Congress Control Number: 2017913142

Print information available on the last page.

WestBow Press rev. date: 9/14/2017

In memory of Mom and her creative, imaginative spirit.

Contents

ACKNOWLEDGMENTS

I would be remiss if I did not initially begin with thanking God for this book. It is a direct reflection of frequent presence in the Word, time and prayer. It is amazing what God can do through humans. I also wish to thank the staff and congregation of First United Methodist Church: first, for trusting me with the task of teaching the Bible to third graders; second, for putting up with my experiments on their children; and third, for providing me with encouragement along the way.

I would like to thank my friends and family and in particular, my loving husband, Ross, and our sons, Samuel and Isaac. Thank you guys for allowing Mom to write when I should have been cooking.

Finally, a big thank-you to the people of Westbow Press for their patience and constant presence as I took the very scary leap of launching this first vessel into the world.

Chapter 1

Awaken the Wonder

Put yourself in the shoes of a modern grade-school child and take a long, critical look at the Bible sitting on your coffee table. The print is small, the language is weird, and there are very few—if any—pictures. Now glance at your favorite handheld device or gaming system and ask yourself which one seems more interesting, exciting, and immediately applicable. The answer is the Bible! *Right?*

In recent years, several terrific resources have been created to bring individual Bible stories to life. The lessons in this book place the spotlight directly on the Bible itself. What is the Bible? Who is the Bible about? What does the Bible contain? Who wrote the Bible? Why was it written? How did the Bible become the book we know today?

The goal of each lesson is to awaken the visual, kinesthetic, and tactile parts of children, to kindle a fire that will ultimately pull them into the Bible for answers that are relevant to their lives. My mission is to make the Bible a familiar and fun place to visit, to awaken the visual and physical feast contained within the words, and to make those words come alive.

This book is the first of a three-part series of lessons designed to awaken the spirit of the Bible within an elementary school-age child. For the fullest benefit, children experiencing this curriculum should be of the age where they enjoy chapter books or are at least familiar with the concept. This curriculum was developed with a third-grade audience in mind but could be used for slightly younger or older audiences. It is perfect in combination with the receipt of a child's first Bible.

Painting Pictures

Visual people respond to color, maps, and pictures. The contents of the Bible primarily focus on what is happening or on a philosophical message. It is often up to the reader to fill in the colors, images, and topography of the stories. This is easy if you are living in the environment where the Bible story took place. It is not so easy when the culture you are most familiar with is as similar to Bible times as an avatar is to a corncob doll.

Consider a passage that relates an absolutely spellbinding story about Samson in the Old Testament.

> When he came to Lehi, the Philistines came shouting to meet him; and the Spirit of the LORD came mightily upon him, and the ropes which were on his arms became as flax that has caught fire, and his bonds melted off his hands. And he found a fresh jawbone of an ass, and put out his hand and seized it, and with it he slew a thousand men. (Judges 15:14–15)

In this story, the Bible uses two brief sentences—just under seventy words—to describe an action sequence in which a bound Samson escapes his captors, hunts around, finds the jawbone of a donkey carcass, and uses it in what must have been an impressive attack on one thousand men. Read that again: one *thousand* men. Today, these fifty-four words would occupy at least fifteen minutes of riveting screen action. The Bible's version is so short that if someone doesn't stop and point it out, the reader might miss it.

Tasting Words

Young children pick up leaves, rocks, and blades of grass, touching the world to see how it feels. The youngest of these children even put the world in their mouths—much to the chagrin of their microbial-minded parents. These children are learning by experience.

People who learn by experience engage all five senses in a task. They *live* the lesson. Experts call this kind of learning kinesthetic and tactual. If you are teaching children, I think it is safe to say you are in the kinesthetic and tactual-experience business.

Recreating the world of the Bible using the senses is key to opening the message and contents of the Bible to a child. Your job as a teacher is to pull back the curtains of the Bible so the individual child can see the colors, feel the wind, and taste the salty sea of God's story. You will know you've succeeded when the child decides to step through the curtain and experience the story on his or her own.

As a result of completing these lessons, children will have a better grasp of the beauty, action, and beating heart of the book we call *Biblia Sacra* (the Holy Bible). You have the privilege of being the person who awakens this wonder within the children you teach. Thank you for reviving the relevance as well as the reverence of this dearly beloved book.

Nuts and Bolts: How to Use this Book

Each lesson has six standard elements.

Prepare

When Paul wrote to the Ephesians about equipping themselves for missionary work, he used the image of armor: the belt of truth, the breastplate of righteousness, the shield of faith, and the helmet of salvation. There's one more piece of equipment: the Word of God.

Paul described the Word as the sword of the spirit (see Ephesians 6:10–18). Think about that. The Word of God is a *sword!* Wielding a sword is not a sedentary activity. Are you ready to spear the hearts and minds of the children you are teaching?

Each chapter begins with a section that will arm you for battle—a meditation to focus your heart and mind on the task before you. This spiritual practice—this battle cry—will provide you with a visual focus on what each lesson is attempting to achieve.

Memory Verse

Each new section of the Bible is introduced with a memory verse, which is designed to encapsulate the essence of the theme for each section. The verse serves two purposes. First, it helps the child focus on the most important concept for the group of books under discussion. Second, the exercise of systematically repeating the same verse fixes it in the child's memory.

By the end of your time together, you will have had the opportunity to plant three strong, wonderful sentences from God into the minds of each child who has been touched by these lessons. The verse and an outside-of-class idea for making it part of each child's experience is included.

Objectives

Objectives are the concrete goals for each lesson. Combined with your visionary work in the preparation stage, the objectives provide you with pathways to arrive at your destination. Each activity is grounded in these statements.

Activities

Every group of children is different. Even if it is the same group of children each time, they will behave differently on different days. What is going on in each child's mind, what each child ate (or didn't eat) for a meal, and who each child interacted with before gracing your door, all play a part in creating the psychological and emotional mood of the group.

Flexibility is the key to unlocking an engaging lesson. Good teachers have a big bag of tricks. Options give teachers the ability to call an audible or change the activity and refocus the group.

Each lesson comes with several different activities that meet the objectives. There will be more provided than you will need or can use. Don't be afraid to switch things up if children aren't having fun. Activities that will work great with any lesson are located in the final chapter of the book.

Prayer/Closing

Sitting quietly in a circle with heads bowed is a valid prayer discipline. *Always* sitting quietly in a circle with heads bowed can also frustrate the more rambunctious members of your group as well as limit their experiences with different types of prayer. Not everyone prays in this way. Not everyone prays the same way every time.

Find a balance and don't forget to teach ways of praying that are meaningful to every individual and not just the quiet ones. Each lesson contains a brief, closing prayer as well as ideas that will help you implement a variety of ways to pray in your classroom.

PARENT CONNECTION

The relief pitcher, the twelfth man, the sidekick—all of these are ways to think about the parents of the children in your class. Help parents help you. Each lesson contains a suggestion on how to invite parents to reinforce what you discuss at home. Who knows? Maybe you will end up reaching more than just the young soul in your class.

TIPS AND HINTS

Resource tips and discussion hints are included throughout the lessons. They are designed to spark your creativity and to help you think outside of the box. These tips should be used to enhance your experience as well as the experiences of the children you are serving. Additional resources, which are great to have in the classroom and support all the lessons, are included at the end of the book.

Note: In the spirit of tips, here is one. Carefully consider the Bible translation you will use to teach your class. With the exception of one verse, which just doesn't sound right in any other but the King James Version, the Revised Standard Version of the Bible is used throughout this book. This was done for practical reasons and primarily because of copyright law. However, my favorite translation to use in my Sunday school class is the Common English Version. Take your time and explore different translations. Use one you feel is written in an understandable language for children yet remains faithful to the spirit of the words.

READY, SET, GO!

Thank you for deciding to engage in the important work of teaching the Bible to a child or group of children. Armed with the tools in this book, go, my friends. Carry out your important work. Awaken a child's wonder at what is contained within the pages of the Bible. Help the children you serve to see the Bible through your eyes, your words, and your actions.

> Go therefore and make disciples of all nations, baptizing them in the name of the Father and of the Son and of the Holy Spirit. (Matthew 28:19)

CHAPTER 2

WHAT IS THE BIBLE? HOW DID IT START?

PREPARE

Thy word is a lamp unto my feet, and a light unto my path.—Psalm 119:105 (KJV)

The words are familiar and even comforting. You probably finished the sentence with your memory rather than your eyes. You may have known those particular words are from the King James Version of Psalms. You may have known the chapter and verse, where they can be found, without looking. You may have hummed the melody to the song "Thy Word," which was made popular by Amy Grant. But when was the last time you read the words and *felt* the message they contained.

Let's try. Relax, sit back, and read the next few paragraphs slowly and carefully with an open and visual mind. Focus your effort on creating mental pictures of what these words describe.

You open your eyes and cannot see. Everything is black. The air around you is steady and cool like it is in a tunnel, a cave, or a cellar. You breathe deeply and smell dirt—the way it smells earthy after a rain. The air's moisture lingers on your skin. You feel the air moving ever so slightly and ever so quietly. All is silent—so silent you feel a slight pressure on your ears.

You know you are underground and in the dark. You fight to control the fear. You force your brain to process how to find a way out.

You tentatively reach sideways with your right hand. Every inch of your body is tense and waiting. Your brain commands your hand to slowly inch its way further to the side, hoping it will find something familiar.

Finally, the tips of your fingers hit something solid. Surprised, you jerk them back. Then you move them forward again. This time you are a little bit surer of the distance between you and whatever you just touched.

You reach and feel the solid side of an earthen wall. The dirt is smooth and cool. You push gently and tentatively, and it holds. Keeping your balance with your feet and legs, you push harder, and it still holds.

Placing your full weight on the wall and using your right hand for leverage, you begin a similar process with your right foot. Not too far in front of you, your foot encounters an object. You tap it gently with the toe of your shoe. Almost immediately, something on the floor starts to glow. Relieved, your eyes feast on the light.

You bend forward slightly and see a book with letters on it. As you focus on it, two words become clear: Holy Bible. Letting go of the wall and squatting down, you reach for the book on the ground. Your hands close around the leather sides of a familiar cover. You feel its weight in your hands and through your arms.

As you stare at it, beams of light leak out from the closed pages. Soon the light reveals your hands, your arms, your bent knees, and your feet. The light shoots forward, and your eyes follow it, drinking in your surroundings. You are in a narrow, earthen tunnel, and there is a door at the end of it with a broken, red sign that says, "Exit."

PRAYER

Sing along with the YouTube video of "Thy Word" written and performed by Amy Grant and Michael W. Smith http://www.youtube.com/watch?v=gs-aiQ9NZ1g.

MEMORY VERSE

Hear, O Israel: The LORD our God is one LORD; and you shall love the LORD your God with all your heart, and with all your soul, and with all your might. (Deuteronomy 6:4–5)

OBJECTIVES

1. Learn the definition of the word *Bible*.
2. Count how many books are in the Bible.
3. Divide the Bible into two parts.
4. Experience a Bible story.

ACTIVITIES

AN EAR TO HEAR

The first phrase of the memory verse tells Israel *to hear*. If it's a nice day, take the group outside and practice *listening*. Have the children sit in a circle and tell them to shut their eyes and sit quietly for thirty seconds. While they are sitting, tell them to listen. When thirty seconds are up, ask them what they heard.

Bonus: Tell them you'd like them to practice listening at home. Ask them to listen this week each day for one to two minutes and to write down what they hear. After the seventh day, have them pick the best thing they heard.

HOW MANY BOOKS?

Prepare: Place sixty-six books in a pile on the floor and several copies of the Bible on a table.

Explain: Ask the children to count the books on the floor and to tell you how many are in the pile. When finished or at the same time if you have a big group, hand out the Bibles and tell the children to count the number of books in a Bible's table of contents.

Ask: Is the number of books on the floor the same as the number of books in the Bible?

Tip: Do you need to find sixty-six books fast? Check out your church library for a set of commentaries or make and use Bible flash cards. Actual books make a bigger visual impression. Do you have more time? Create a set of *books* you can use over and over again by purchasing sixty-six equally-sized food boxes (macaroni and cheese, fruit snacks, cereal) and make a set of books of the Bible. Use duct tape to reinforce and strengthen the boxes and then double wrap each box in wrapping paper. Decorate and label them as desired.

Laying the Foundation			A Promise Fulfilled			The Birth of the Church		
Law	Old History	Poetry and Wisdom Literature	Major Prophets	Minor Prophets	Gospels	New History	Paul's Letters to Churches	Epistles and Revelation
Genesis	Joshua	Job	Isaiah	Hosea	Matthew	Acts	Romans	Hebrews
Exodus	Judges	Psalms	Jeremiah	Joel	Mark		1 Corinthians	James
Leviticus	Ruth	Proverbs	Lamentations	Amos	Luke		2 Corinthians	1 Peter
Numbers	1 Samuel	Ecclesiastes	Ezekiel	Obadiah	John		Galatians	2 Peter
Deuteronomy	2 Samuel	Song of Solomon	Daniel	Jonah			Ephesians	1 John
	1 Kings			Micah			Philippians	2 John
	2 Kings			Nahum			Colossians	3 John
	1 Chronicles			Habakkuk			1 Thessalonians	Jude
	2 Chronicles			Zephaniah			2 Thessalonians	Revelation
	Ezra			Haggai			1 Timothy	
	Nehemiah			Zechariah			2 Timothy	
	Esther			Malachi			Titus	
							Philemon	

Look It Up

Prepare: Find and place a children's dictionary, an American English dictionary, or tablet or phone, which is connected to the Internet, on the table.

Explain: Have the children look up the words *Bible* and *testament* and share what they find. If there is more than one dictionary or resource, have a race to see who can find the word the fastest.

Ask: What does each word mean?

What Does the Word *Bible* Mean?

Prepare: Write the words, "The Holy Bible," on a whiteboard, chalkboard, or flip chart.

Ask: You have probably learned in school that words have meanings. Can you guess what the word *Bible* might mean?

Explain: The word *Bible* means books. The Bible is a book of books that was written over a long period of time (1,600 years) by many different people. The word comes from a Latin word: *biblia*, which means any large book. In Latin, holy books are called *Biblia Sacra*. People who speak English shorten the word to Bible and use the word when talking about the Christian Bible—God's Holy Book. The Bible is actually sixty-six smaller books squished together into one big book or *biblia*.

Hint: *Biblia Sacra* is pronounced "BIB-lee-ah SAK-rah."

One Book, Two Parts

Prepare: Write the word *Testament* on a whiteboard, chalkboard, or flip chart

Explain: Give each child a copy of the Bible. Tell the children to find the table of contents and to look for the word *Testament*.

Ask: How many *Testament* words can you find? What comes before the word *Testament*? What do the words *old* and *new* mean? What do you think the word *testament* means? Why do you think they were called the *Old* and *New* Testaments?

Hint: The point of this exercise is to allow children to discover the meaning on their own by asking them questions to help them get there. This method of inquiry and discussion was used by Socrates to help his students learn and is called the Socratic method.

Ask the children questions to help them remember that the Bible is a book of books. The books are divided into two main groups: the Old Testament and the New Testament.

The word *testament* means words that are used as evidence to support a fact. A testament is a symbol of an agreement about truth—a promise.

The Old Testament contains books that tell about the relationship between God and his people before Jesus was born. The New Testament contains books that tell about the relationship between God and his people after Jesus was born.

Bible Book Sorting Game

Prepare: Get or make a deck of Bible Book flash cards. Shuffle the cards so they are mixed up and out of order. Place them in the middle of a table.

Explain: Using the Bible's table of contents as a reference, the kids must divide the decks of cards into two piles—one pile each for the Old Testament and one pile for the New Testament. If you have enough supplies, give each child a deck and let the children race each other.

Tip: Free, downloadable templates for business card-sized flash cards are available online. Consider printing them in color for the best effect. Use different colors for each Bible book group: the law, history, poetry, wisdom literature, major prophets, minor prophets, the gospels, Acts, Paul's letters, the Epistles, and Revelation. Larger sized templates are also available or can be easily made and printed.

Around the Campfire

Prepare: Place a makeshift campfire in the middle of the floor with plenty of room to sit around it. A campfire can be made of something as simple as a pile of wooden blocks or as elaborate as a tablet with a streaming picture of a campfire. Make sure your special guest(s) have been invited and know what to do.

Ask: Has anyone ever been camping? What is it like to camp? Has anyone ever heard or told a story before bed or while sitting around a campfire?

Explain: The Bible wasn't always written down. When it started, it was a collection of stories passed down from adults to the children, which taught them about God and their family history. The people who told these stories (storytellers) were trained to do so, and their job was very important. The storyteller had to remember all the details exactly as they had happened. The old storytellers would choose and train new storytellers so the stories would continue to be passed down forever. A person could become a storyteller only after they had spent many, many years learning from an elder.

Special Guest: Invite older people in the church to tell the children the story of when they received their first Bibles. Ask them to talk about their childhoods and what they remember about being in grade school. Ask them to discuss what the Bible has meant to them over the years. Ask them to tell the children about their favorite Bible story.

Tip: This is a great opportunity for campfire-themed snacks such as s'mores, beef jerky, or fruit jerky.

PRAYER/CLOSING

Prepare: Write the memory verse on a whiteboard, chalkboard, or flip chart and place it in a prominent spot in the room, preferably in a place where it can remain for a while.

Explain: Teach the children how to say the memory verse with the actions. Repeat the verse together several times. Use the final time as your closing prayer.

Verse	Action
Hear, O Israel: The LORD our God is one LORD;	Raise your hands to cup your ears.
and you shall love the LORD your God with all your heart,	Place your hands over your heart.
and with all your soul,	Stretch your arms out.
and with all your might.	Strike a muscleman's pose.
Deuteronomy 6:4–5	Show the numbers in the scripture with your fingers as you say them.

PARENT CONNECTION

TAKE THE MEMORY VERSE HOME

One of the best ways to involve parents is to have them work on the memory verses with their children. Each memory verse spans four lessons. Each lesson focuses on one part of the memory verse. In this lesson, focus on the first two sentences of this verse.

Some versions of the Bible put exclamation points after each sentence. Heads up, people! We are to listen! Give the children listening homework. Encourage them to pay attention to sounds they hear as they move through each day. Which day sounded the best? Write a note to the parents encouraging them to help their child listen.

PARENT LETTER

Start the lessons off right by sending a letter to parents introducing yourself and your passion for the Bible. Introduce the topic for the next few lessons and help them prepare for the class ahead. Explain the active nature of the class so children can dress appropriately. If snacks will be served, ask about allergies. Finally, call parents to action. Invite parents to join social media groups for your class or give them instructions for submitting their email addresses so you can communicate with them more frequently.

SOCIAL MEDIA

Consider harnessing the power of social media outlets like Facebook and Twitter. Closed Facebook pages require an invitation and an approval to join. Open Facebook pages do not require an invitation and can be *liked* by anyone who uses Facebook.

There are a few protocols with open pages that you will need to clear in advance. First, make sure the church administration approves of communication to parents in this way. They may prefer guiding parents to the church website instead. They may have additional rules you must follow. Never post pictures or names of individual children on a public site without the express, written permission of the child's parent. Used properly, social media can be a powerful communication tool.

Chapter 3
God Starts Small

Genesis

Prepare

> I see a star; You see the Milky Way.—Lyric from "Who but You" by Mark Hall and Megan Garrett

When was the last time you drove out to the country, lay in the back of your pickup truck or on the hood of your car, and gazed at the stars? If you have time, do it. Go have some quality *star* time.* While you are pondering the vastness of the universe, think about the words God spoke to Abraham.

> And he brought him outside and said, "Look toward heaven, and number the stars, if you are able to number them." Then he said to him, "So shall your descendants be." (Genesis 15:5)

It must have been difficult for Abraham to imagine the impact he and his family would have on the world. Abraham and Sarah were in their nineties when Sarah gave birth to their first and only son, Isaac. We know they were thrilled with the miracle of birth because they were at such an advanced age. We also know Abraham was a man of faith. He believed God would do as he promised. But I think even Abraham would be surprised to see the immeasurable impact his family has had upon the modern world.

As the lyrics in the song "Who but You" indicate, Abraham saw a star. God sees the Milky Way. There are many stories in the Bible, but the story of Abraham is one that clearly illustrates the vast difference between a human point of view and God's. Just as Abraham could not possibly have foreseen that his family tree would eventually produce the Messiah—the Savior of the world—there is no way we can fully imagine God's plan for the world.

God is indeed awesome. God is indeed magnificent. God is indeed wonderful. God is indeed good.

Read the first five books of the Bible to see the early parts of this master plan. It's a place where we can watch God at work through the actions of Christianity's first family. Though we may not be direct descendants of Abraham, his story is still our story. Anyone who believes Jesus Christ is his or her risen Savior roots his or her faith in the family of Abraham, Sarah, and Isaac—real people who lived real lives and placed every ounce of their faith in God and his promise.

*If you don't have time to go out or a place nearby to stargaze in, spend time on the Internet searching for images of stars. Some search words would be *galaxy*, *stars*, and *star field*.

Prayer

Prepare for this lesson by listening to the simple but powerful words and music of Michael W. Smith in his song, "Our God is an Awesome God." Check out this video for inspiration and encouragement: http://www.youtube.com/watch?v=38V8jnN1Kpw.

Memory Verse

Hear, O Israel: The LORD our God is one LORD; and you shall love the LORD your God with all your heart, and with all your soul, and with all your might. (Deuteronomy 6:4–5)

Objectives

1. Practice saying the first five books of the Bible aloud.
2. Learn the different words for the group of books called the Law.
3. Read about the promise God gave to Abraham.

Activities

More than the Stars

Prepare: Copy the star pattern included with the lesson on card stock. Gather glitter glue, glitter crayons, neon markers, and gel pens. Place everything on a table.

Explain: Using the craft supplies, decorate the star, taking care not to cover the Bible verse.

When they are finished, punch a hole in the tops of their stars and tie pieces of yarn through the holes. Place them out of the way to dry. Tell the children to hang their stars up at home to remind them of God's promise to Abraham.

Ask: What does the word *descendant* mean?

Hint: To help the kids figure out the meaning of the word descendant, explain that children are descendants of their parents. Then tell them they are also descendants of their grandparents. Enjoy this conversation while decorating the stars.

Abraham,
your descendants
will be like the
stars –
too many to
count!

THREE NAMES FOR THE LAW

Prepare: Place the first five books of the Bible on a table—either the flash cards, the Bible books you have created, or the table of contents in the child's Bible. On a whiteboard, chalkboard, or flip chart, write the words Pentateuch, Torah, and law.

Explain: The first five books of the Bible are the oldest ones. Bible scholars believe these books were all written by a man named Moses. The books are grouped together. The group of books is called the Pentateuch. Pentateuch means "five containers." In the Hebrew language, the language Jesus spoke, the books were called the Torah, which means law or instruction.

These books have been around for a long time. They contain the story of the Creation, Noah and the great flood, Abraham and his family, and the Ten Commandments. Lots of people, including Jesus, have read and studied these five books and the words they contain.

If you go to a Jewish church today, you will find these books kept separate from the rest of the Bible and printed on a scroll. They may even be written in the Hebrew language.

Reading from the Torah is a very important part of Jewish worship services. Reading from the Bible in a Christian church is an important part of worship. When we read the Bible, we believe the words in it were written by people whom God directly inspired. It's like hearing God speak directly to us.

Some churches have everyone stand up as a sign of respect and attention when the Bible is read aloud. When someone is reading from the Bible, it is a good time to be quiet and to use our ears to listen.

Ask: Do we read from the Bible in our church? Do we read from the Bible at home?

Tip: This is a long but important part of the lesson. One way to make is more visual is to show pictures of the things you are discussing. Use a tablet or a phone to show pictures of a Torah scroll rolled up and unrolled. Some images show close-ups of the Hebrew language being read using a yad—a pointer used to touch the delicate paper of the Torah scroll. You can purchase souvenir-sized versions of the Torah from Jewish church supply stores. Get a church bulletin and use it when discussing times when the Bible is read during a church service.

Hint: Pentateuch is pronounced "PEN-tah-tuke." Say it several times until the children get it right. Yad is pronounced "Yay-d" and means "hand" in Hebrew.

MAP IT: ABRAHAM TRAVELS FROM UR TO CANAAN

Prepare: Find a map of Abraham's travels from Ur to Canaan—the bigger the better. Christian bookstores often have poster-sized maps or books with maps showing Abraham's travels. A map of Abraham's travels can also often be found in the back of a good study Bible.

Explain: The stories in the Bible are real and happened in places that are still around today. We can find these places on a map, travel to them, and walk where the people of the Bible used to walk.

Abraham grew up in a city called Ur (Genesis 11:27–29). Ur is in Babylon, located close to the Persian Gulf. Abraham's father decided to move his family to Canaan. So they left Ur and went north around the mountains but decided to stop instead at Haran (Genesis 11:31). Haran is in Assyria, north of Canaan, about one hundred miles inland from the Mediterranean Sea. After living for a long time in Haran, the Lord told Abraham to continue on to Canaan (Genesis 12:1–6). Canaan is now Israel. Canaan is where the family lived when the story we are about to read happened.

Ask: What is Canaan called today? Can you imagine packing up and moving your whole family to a strange city because God told you to do it?

Hint: Ur is pronounced "ER." Haran is pronounced "HAIR-uhn" like Karen. Canaan is pronounced "KAY-nuhn."

Tip: You will be covering a lot of territory with this explanation, but it is critical in order to set the stage for the next lesson. It is important to know the story well in order to summarize it quickly for the children and to keep them interested. To show the children how Abraham and his family lived, use a tablet or your phone to research images of ancient, nomadic desert life.

Look It Up: The Binding of Isaac

Prepare: Write Genesis 22:1–18 on a whiteboard, chalkboard, or flip chart. Make sure there is one Bible for each child, preferably all the same Bible or, at the very minimum, the same translation.

Explain: The words and numbers on this page are called a "Bible verse reference." It's like a map of how to find something in the Bible. These Bible verses tell an important story about God and Abraham. We are going to go on a treasure hunt to find the verses and to read the story.

Ask: How many of you have heard this story before? What did God tell Abraham to do? Why didn't Abraham sacrifice Isaac? Why was God impressed with Abraham? What did God promise to Abraham as a result? What is a descendant? How many descendants will Abraham have? Where will his descendants live? Was it fun looking up verses in the Bible?

Hint: For many, this will be the very first time they have ever looked up a verse in the Bible. Take your time and make sure everyone is getting it. Break the Bible reference into parts and look each part up together. Looking up the book is a perfect place to show the Bible's table of contents.

Children in early elementary school are familiar with the concept of books with chapters. It helps to point out that chapter numbers in the Bible are larger and are within the text as well as at the top of the page.

A verse might be a new concept. It will help to compare it to the main text and to explain that the numbers are there but are smaller. Also explain that when they are looking up verses, they have to be careful not to start reading the next chapter. You may have to explain that verse 1 typically does not have a 1 by it and that numbering usually starts with the number 2.

The First Three Stars in the Sky

Prepare: You will need a blank wall, a large sheet of paper, or a large whiteboard. You will be using this board for the entire series so make sure it is big enough to hold all the parts. The bigger the board is the better. For this lesson, create three stars using the template in the back of the book—one for Abraham, one for Sarah, and one for Isaac. See the final page for an example of a completed star wall and star template.

Explain: God chose Abraham to start a family of people who would serve and worship Him as the one, true God. God protected Abraham's family so it would grow. Everything God promised Abraham came true. Eventually, Abraham's family was so big, they became a nation of people called the Israelites. It is important to remember that this huge nation of people started with just one small family of three—Abraham, his wife, Sarah, and their son, Isaac.

Hint: The stars for Abraham, Sarah, and Isaac can either be placed on the wall ahead of time or hung on the wall interactively as you talk about the family.

Prayer/Closing

Prepare: If you want the children to lead the prayer, write the verses on pieces of paper.

Explain: This prayer is said as an echo prayer. With heads bowed and hands folded, the leader says a sentence, and the children repeat the same sentence.

You can either have one leader read the entire prayer or give each child part of the prayer and let him or her take turns being the leader.

1. Thank you, God, for your promise to Abraham.
2. Thank you, God, for allowing me into Abraham's family.
3. I have listened.
4. You are my only Lord.
5. I will love you with all my heart.
6. I will love you with all my being.
7. I will love you with all my strength.
8. Forgive me when I do not love you.
9. Forgive me when I do not listen.
10. In Jesus's name we pray, amen.

PARENT CONNECTION

TAKE THE MEMORY VERSE HOME

Prepare: (optional) Gather enough simple greeting cards so each child has five to take home or make your own "I Love You" note cards from business card-sized templates.

Explain: This lesson, focus on what it means to love God with your heart. One way to show people we love them is to tell them. Tell God you love him by practicing the memory verse every day or by telling him you love him in prayer. Another way to show God you love him is to share love with others. Give an "I Love You" card to someone special each day. Make sure you give one to the person who brings you to church, because that person is helping you learn more about God.

CHAPTER 4
MORE THAN THE STARS

GENESIS

PREPARE

In this lesson, we explore a pivotal story in the Bible. The story of Jacob and his sons is in Genesis for a reason. It is the story of how Jacob changed his name to Israel. It's the story of how something bad can be morphed by God into something ultimately good. It is the story of how the twelve tribes of Israel originated. It's the story of how the Israelites ended up in Egypt. It's the story of a father's love for his son. It's the story of a son's love for his family. It's the story of youthful error. It's the story of human failure. It's the story of forgiveness throughout time. All these messages are located in one story—the story of Abraham's grandson and great-grandsons.

This epic story originates when God makes a covenant with Abraham in Genesis 17. It follows the family and its escapades to the time when it lands in Egypt under the care of Joseph in Genesis 47. The more you read about this family, the more you may wonder why. The family in this story lies, brags, tricks, connives, gossips, gets angry, fights, and is jealous of one another's belongings. If closets come with skeletons, this closet has its fair share.

But wait a minute, this is the family God chose to carry out his plan! Aren't the people God chooses supposed to be perfect? What made God choose these people out of everyone else who was available?

The Bible answers these questions by pointing us right back to Grandfather Abraham. God chose Abraham because he was faithful to God. For one thing, Abraham did everything God asked him to do like move all over the Middle Eastern countryside with his friends and family. Abraham put God and his plan first. Abraham also trusted God even when God said unbelievable things like telling him he would have a large family even though he was very old and had no children.

This is the kind of faith God desires from us—complete and utter trust and acceptance of his plan for our lives. When we allow God to lead, God can accomplish phenomenal things through us despite our imperfections.

In what is considered his finest hymn, Joachim Neander wrote, "Praise ye the Lord! O let all that is in me adore him!" Abraham accomplished this task. With Abraham's example before us, let's watch God as he keeps his promise. Let's remember the story of Abraham, Isaac, Jacob, and his sons with our whole body—with all of our life and breath. Like Abraham, let's find ways to engage our entire being and all of our soul. Let's move together. Let's lift our voices together. Let's marvel in the things God can do when we put him firmly in charge.

Prayer

Read Psalm 148 quietly to yourself. Next read Psalm 148 out loud with your inside voice. Then I triple dog dare you to read Psalm 148 with your outside voice. Shout it! Shout it out loud. Feel the words vibrate in your chest and lungs. Let your voice be heard.

Memory Verse

Hear, O Israel: The LORD our God is one LORD; and you shall love the LORD your God with all your heart, and with all your soul, and with all your might. (Deuteronomy 6:4–5)

Objectives

1. Practice putting the first five books of the Bible in order.
2. Find Canaan and Egypt on a Bible map.
3. Hear the stories of Jacob and Joseph.

Activities

Shout It Out!

Prepare: Make sure the memory verse is in a place where the children can see it.

Explain: Tell the children to work on the memory verse by saying it in different ways: tiny voice, whispered voice, outside voice, inside voice, shouting voice, army voice, wavy voice, etc. Repeat the verse until you are bored. You are limited only by time, imagination, and creativity.

Look It Up: Inheritance for a Bowl of Soup

Prepare: Write Genesis 25:19–34 on a whiteboard, chalkboard, or flip chart. Make sure everyone gets his or her own Bible verse, preferably from the same Bible or, at the very minimum, from the same translation. Make three more stars, by using the template in the back of the book, to add to the wall: Rebecca, Esau, and Jacob.

Explain: Isaac grew up in Canaan with his family. When it came time for him to get married, he traveled back to Haran to look for a wife. Isaac married a woman named Rebekah. Rebekah and Isaac had twin boys.

In Bible times, when a father dies, all of his property and land typically are given to the firstborn son. Of the two boys, Esau was born first. Jacob was born holding onto his brother's heel. Today's story is about these two boys. Practice looking up the new code together using the tips you learned in the last lesson. Read the story of Esau and Jacob.

Ask: Why did Isaac like Esau? Why do you suppose Rebekah liked Jacob? What did Esau give to Jacob in exchange for a bowl of stew? What is a birthright?

Hint: Esau's name is pronounced "EE-saw." Leah's name is pronounced "LEE-ah."

God's Promise: More than the Stars

Prepare: Make fourteen stars using the star template at the back of the book: Leah, Rachel, and all of their sons. You will put these stars on the wall in order from oldest to youngest: Reuben, Simeon, Levi, Judah, Dan, Naphtali, Issachar, Zebulun, Gad, Asher, Joseph, Benjamin. The rest of the lessons will trace all descendants back to one of the twelve brothers.

Explain: After Isaac died, Jacob got all of his father's property and land because of the agreement they made over the bowl of soup. When it was time to get married, Jacob went north again to find a wife from the place his mother came from—Haran.

There Jacob met two sisters. He immediately fell in love with Rachel, the younger of the two. When he got ready to marry her, Rachel's father tricked him into marrying her older sister, Leah, instead.

When Jacob figured out whom he had married, he was really mad. He made a deal with Leah's father to work additional years in order to marry Rachel as well. Sometime after he had married Rachel, he took Leah, Rachel, and the rest of his family back to Canaan to live. The family raised twelve boys there (Genesis 24:61–35:18).

Ask: How many people were in Abraham's family when it began? How many people were in Abraham's family at the end of the story? What was the promise God made to Abraham? Is God keeping his promise to Abraham?

Hint: It is important to know the story well in order to summarize it quickly for the children and to keep them interested. This story also contains some tricky parts. For example, Jacob essentially had four wives. To minimize this distraction, the exercise ignores Zilpah's and Bilhah's parts in the story.

To explain Jacob's marriage to two wives, I've found that a practical, simple explanation works best. In the old days, it was common for men to have more than one wife. Big families were necessary to do the work involved to keep people alive.

The more difficult brothers' names are pronounced this way: Reuben is "ROO-bin," Simeon is "SIM-ee-uhn," Naphtali is "NAF-tuh-lie," Issachar is "ISS-u-kar," Zebulun is "ZEH-byoo-luhn," and Asher is "ASH-er."

Map It: From Canaan to Egypt

Prepare: Find a map showing Canaan and Egypt. The bigger it is the better. Christian bookstores often have poster-sized maps or books with maps showing the pilgrimage of Abraham's family from Ur to Egypt. A map of the family's travels is also often found in the back of a good study Bible.

Ask: How many of you have heard the story of Joseph and his many-colored coat? What happened?

Explain: See if the children know any parts of the story of Joseph and his brothers and fill in the gaps. Joseph was Rachel's son and Jacob's favorite. Jacob treated Joseph in special ways and gave him special things. To make matters worse, Joseph bragged about how he dreamed that his brothers would eventually serve him. So the brothers plotted to get rid of Joseph and sold him to some people taking slaves down to Egypt.

Joseph was sold to a rich man and quickly became a trusted servant. Unfortunately, the rich man's wife also liked Joseph. When he wouldn't do what she wanted, she got her husband to throw Joseph in prison. He stayed there until Pharaoh started having disturbing dreams about skinny cows eating fat cows.

Joseph could interpret dreams. He told Pharaoh that there would be a famine in the land and that they should prepare for it by storing food. Pharaoh made Joseph his right-hand man. Joseph became an important figure in Egypt.

Sure enough, seven years of famine struck the land and even reached all the way to Canaan. Joseph's brothers heard there was food in Egypt and traveled there to get some for their families to eat. They did not recognize Joseph at first, but Joseph recognized them. After he played some tricks on them to make sure they were sorry for what they had done, he told them who he was, forgave them, and had them move the entire family to Egypt so everyone would survive. The brothers went back home to get Jacob, Leah, and the rest of the family and moved to Egypt where they served Pharaoh (Genesis 37:1–47:12).

Tip: In this lesson, we take Jacob's family from Canaan all the way to Egypt. It is important to know the story well in order to summarize it quickly for the children and to keep them interested. One fun way to tell this story is to show the YouTube video of the prologue to *Joseph and the Amazing Technicolor Dreamcoat*, starring Donny Osmond. It's colorful, and it does a good job of summarizing the story of the brothers.

Prayer/Closing

Prepare: Place the verse in a prominent spot in the room so the children can see it.

Ask: Does anyone remember the actions we did with our last memory verse?

Explain: Read the Bible memory verse and do the actions. See if the children can remember it with their eyes closed. Repeat the verse together as a prayer, putting actions with the words. Repeat as many as three times, complete the actions, and alternate the volume (whisper, inside voice, outside voice).

Verse	Action
Hear, O Israel: The LORD our God is one LORD;	Raise your hands to cup your ears.
and you shall love the LORD your God with all your heart,	Place your hands over your heart.
and with all your soul,	Stretch your arms out.
and with all your might.	Strike a muscleman's pose.
Deuteronomy 6:4–5 (RSV)	Show the numbers in the scripture with your fingers as you say them.

Parent Connection

Take the Memory Verse Home

Prepare: Gather six stickers per child.

Explain: Share a little joyful noise at home. Shout the verse from memory at least six times. Each time the child completes the verse successfully, give him or her one sticker in honor of completing it.

Tip: You might want to send a note home with the children about what is happening in class. Involve parents so the stickers don't end up on furniture or somewhere they shouldn't go.

Chapter 5
A Nation of Followers

Exodus, Leviticus, Numbers, and Deuteronomy

Prepare

The story of the Israelite Exodus from Egypt is the perfect scenario for a reality television series or a strategy-based video game. I can see the preview now.

Shanghaied in Sinai

> You have been turned loose in the desert with six hundred thousand of your nearest friends and family. They need a leader, and that leader is you! Your task? Nurture, raise, and train an army prepared to conquer Canaan in forty years.

When confronted with the actual scope of the job God asked Moses to do, we can understand, more fully, his reluctance to do it. Shepherding six hundred thousand people and their belongings through several hundred miles of desert just sounds *hard*. Thanks anyway, God, but I think I have to wash my hair that day. The closest thing we have to something like this is agreeing to run for mayor of a large, metropolitan city. I think we can all agree this is a job for which only a select few are qualified.

There is a reason why Moses is one of the most beloved Hebrew ancestors of all time. There is a reason people attribute the first five books of the Bible to him. There is a reason he was one of the few people God spoke with directly. This guy was a superstar—an avenger! He could easily join the Justice League. He even had God-given superpowers. I stand today in awe of his leadership and his example.

So what happened after Moses and God pull out all the stops to perform some pretty amazing feats for Pharaoh's enjoyment? They took this nation of wandering people and created an orderly, well-oiled society. How did they do it? With rules and with protocol.

I've always been the annoying kid who asks, "Why?" when confronted with a rule I don't understand. But I have grown to realize that some rules are necessary—even rules I don't agree with.

Some rules are simply required if a large body of people is to function properly. The Israelites were too numerous to manage things in the way that had worked up to that point. They needed structure. So God delivered an outstanding and timeless framework of rules to Moses from which to start.

God gave Moses the basic major outline or the overarching policy, and Moses filled in the details, the regulations, and the case laws. Together, God and Moses made a terrific team. They saved Israel from slavery and kept a nation of people alive for forty years. At the end of those forty years, they brought this nation from the desert to the outer edge of the Promised Land. Thank you, God, for rules.

One of the reasons I love Deuteronomy is because it contains three of Moses's speeches—his words. When I read Deuteronomy, I like to picture Moses on my couch, hanging out and chatting with me. With this image in mind, read Deuteronomy 5:2–22 and 6:1–9.

Prayer

As your class has been doing for the past four lessons, pray the words of the Hebrew Shema.

> Hear, O Israel: The LORD our God is one LORD; and you shall love the LORD your God with all your heart, and with all your soul, and with all your might. (Deuteronomy 6:4–5)

Memory Verse

> Hear, O Israel: The LORD our God is one LORD; and you shall love the LORD your God with all your heart, and with all your soul, and with all your might. (Deuteronomy 6:4–5)

Objectives

1. Connect Moses to Israel's Levite tribe.
2. Find and read the Ten Commandments in Exodus.
3. Review the first five books of the Bible.

Activities

Ten Commandments for Kids

Prepare: Print the Ten Commandments poster on different colored card stock. Gather markers, gel pens, colored pencils, stickers, sequins, and other things that might be fun to decorate with.

Ask: What is written on these posters? Do you know any of these commandments? How did we get the Ten Commandments? Which is the hardest rule to keep? Which is the easiest?

Explain: Have the children pick out one of the Ten Commandments' posters each and tell them to decorate them to hang in their rooms. Show the children how to make easy hangers by taping the two ends of a four by six-inch piece of yarn to the back of their posters using a firm tape such as masking tape or duct tape.

Discuss: While the children are decorating, talk about how Moses had to care for a large group of people living in the desert. God gave Moses a set of ten basic rules to help. Talk about how Moses and the Israelites came up with more rules based on those ten rules. Those rules are found in Numbers and Leviticus. Explain that, by following the rules, the Israelites demonstrated how much they loved God.

The 10 Commandments for Kids

1) Love God more than anything else.
2) Don't make anything in your life more important than God.
3) Always say God's name with respect.
4) Honor the Lord by resting on the seventh day of the week
5) Love and respect your mom and dad.
6) Never hurt anyone.
7) Always be faithful and loyal to members of your family.
8) Don't take anything that isn't yours.
9) Always tell the truth.
10) Be happy with what you have. Don't wish for other people's things.

Exodus 20:1-17 and Deuteronomy 5:4-20

The 10 Commandments for Kids

1) Love God more than anything else.
2) Don't make anything in your life more important than God.
3) Always say God's name with respect.
4) Honor the Lord by resting on the seventh day of the week
5) Love and respect your mom and dad.
6) Never hurt anyone.
7) Always be faithful and loyal to members of your family.
8) Don't take anything that isn't yours.
9) Always tell the truth.
10) Be happy with what you have. Don't wish for other people's things.

Exodus 20:1-17 and Deuteronomy 5:4-20

Look it Up: More than the Stars (Reprise)

Prepare: Write Exodus 1:1–14 on a whiteboard, a large piece of paper, or a flip chart, where everyone can see it. Gather one Bible for each child.

Explain: Find the Bible verse and read the passage together.

Ask: Does anyone remember how the Israelite family ended up in Egypt? Do you remember the name of Jacob's son who was Pharaoh's right-hand man? How big was Jacob's family when they first moved to Egypt? How big did their family grow while they lived there? How is this another example of God staying faithful to what he promised Abraham? Why did the large number of Israelites worry the Egyptians? What did the Egyptians do? How do you suppose God is going to get the Israelites out of this mess?

Moses: A Daring Rescue

Prepare: Gather enough Bibles so there is one per child. The Bible you use should preferably be child friendly and contain headlines that note each plague. If you can't find a Bible with headlines, write the name of each plague on its own index card or piece of paper. Using the star template at the back of the book, make a star for the wall with the name Moses on it. Write the number "600,000" on a colorful piece of paper to hang on the wall or to show at the proper time in the story.

Ask: Who knows the story of Moses? How was Moses raised? Why did Moses leave Egypt? What did Moses find in the desert when he was out tending sheep? Who spoke to Moses through the burning bush? Do you think God speaks to people like this today? What do you think you should do when you are pretty sure God is telling you to do something? How big is six hundred thousand? Who remembers what God promised to Abraham a few lessons back? How many people did Abraham start with in his family? Do you think God is fulfilling his promise to make Abraham the father of a great nation?

Explain: See how much of the Moses story the children know (most likely, quite a bit). When you have finished highlighting the early story of Moses, together, remind the children that it wasn't easy to get Pharaoh to let go of his nation of slaves. Moses, with God's help, had to send plagues on the land of Egypt to get Pharaoh's attention.

Walk the children through each of the plagues by letting them read the headlines in their Bibles or by reading the names of the plagues on their index cards (The plagues start in Exodus 7). Spend time discussing each plague and emphasizing its magnitude and scope.

Before talking about the last plague, explain that none of the previous plagues had worked, so God sent one final and very serious plague. Discuss the final plague in some detail, including God showing the Israelites how to get the Angel of Death to *pass over* their homes by painting lamb's blood on their doors.

Complete the story by saying that the final plague worked and that Moses and the Israelites were allowed to leave Egypt. Tell the children that Moses led six hundred thousand Israelites out of slavery (Exodus 12:37). Show the six hundred thousand template. Talk for a few minutes about how many people six hundred thousand represents to let that number sink in.

The Eleven plagues

1. Turning rods into snakes
2. Turning water into blood
3. Invasion of frogs
4. Swarming lice
5. Swarms of insects
6. Sick and dying animals
7. Skin sores and blisters
8. Hail and thunder
9. Invasion of locusts
10. Darkness over all Egypt
11. Death of every oldest male child

Hint: It is important to know the story well in order to summarize it quickly for the children and to keep them interested. What they don't know is how this story connects to the story of Abraham's family. This is a fun, mind-blowing lesson, if done properly. Help them see the connection between the Israelite people and Moses by explaining that Moses was a descendant of Jacob's son Levi. This is a good time to put Moses's star on the wall or chart to help the children make a visual connection to Abraham's family. Continue by talking about the story of the burning bush and how God spoke to Moses.

Tip: If you know someone with a bug collection, this is a good time to haul it out for show and tell to create an added visual element to the lesson. When explaining large numbers like six hundred thousand, it is important to use concepts that are familiar to children. For example, to get six hundred thousand toasted oats, you will need to have 136 boxes of cereal. If you stack six hundred thousand spaghetti noodles end to end, they will measure 113 miles, which takes over an hour to drive by car.

The Law in Review

Prepare: Gather Bible flash cards or Bible books and separate the first five books from the rest.

Explain: Review the first five books of the Bible and the stories you have covered so far. Besides the Creation story, Genesis contains the story of Abraham, Isaac, Jacob, and Jacob's twelve sons. Exodus is the story of Moses, the Israelites, and their escape (or exit) from Egypt. Leviticus was the Israelites' rulebook. Numbers is the story of what happened during their forty years in the desert and contains rules for worship. Deuteronomy contains speeches from Moses about how to worship God.

Hint: Although this lesson focuses mostly on the story of Exodus, three additional books in the Law were written to explain the Israelites' time in the desert and how they established an early Jewish society. Once the children are hooked on the story of Moses and have connected him to the family of Abraham, you will find they will be very curious about what the rest of the books contain. This is a good sign that you are beginning to reach their minds.

Tip: Play games to memorize the first five books of the Bible. Find game ideas in the final chapter of this book.

Prayer/Closing

Prepare: Place the memory verse in a location where it can be easily seen.

Explain: Have the children sit with their heads bowed, eyes closed, and hands folded or stand in a circle holding hands silently and with heads bowed.

Pray:

> Dear God, thank you for giving us four times to learn more about the book you gave to us. We know you have a plan for us, and you started that plan with Abraham, Sarah, and Isaac. Thank you for staying faithful to your promise to Abraham and for having people pass these stories down to their children so we can read about them today. Be with us. Help us to learn our memory verse to the best of our ability. Forgive us for anything we have done to break your commandments. Help us keep your commandments in the future. Most of all, God, thank you for loving us. Amen.

Parent Connection

Take the Memory Verse Home

Committing a verse to memory takes mental focus and strength. Challenge the children to a *strength* exercise. For this lesson's memory verse, tell them to repeat the verse while doing jumping jacks, skipping, running, or walking. The point is they cannot stand or sit still while saying the verse.

Tip: A visual gift item to add to your at home strength exercise is a tough-looking, temporary, Christian tattoo. Find Christian tattoos online at party supply or novelty stores. You may also be able to find them at your local Christian bookstore.

Chapter 6
We Will Rock You!

Joshua, Judges, and Ruth

Prepare

I think when children hear and speak about the book of Judges in the Bible, they see a guy in a black robe sitting behind a large bench peacefully doling out verdicts of justice. That's about as far as most people get. However, if you dig just a tiny bit further into the facts, the descriptions you read instantly start to contradict that image. Just who were the judges of the Bible?

The closest one to the stereotype was Samuel. His claim to fame was fairly low-key. God spoke to him in a dream while he was working for a priest. He did a lot of talking. He is considered a prophet/judge. At the opposite end of the spectrum is our old friend Samson. He definitely wasn't a talker. Instead, he was a hot head who killed a bunch of people with the jawbone of a donkey.

Gideon, another judge, created all kinds of chaos by destroying altars to Baal and the goddess Asherah. Deborah, the She-Ra Princess of Power of the Bible, led a military counterattack against the king of Canaan and his military general Sisera.

Say what? This is definitely not the docile, sheep and pasture-filled picture I get on an average day in Sunday school. This is cable miniseries stuff. These are tall, buff, muscle-bound men and women with long hair tied back with leather strips wielding broadswords, maces, and spears. There are battle cries and smoke. There is blood and sounds of hand-to-hand combat. Let's face it, by your average boy's standards, the judges were pretty cool.

The books of History are full of acts of military might, and nowhere is that more apparent than the first two books of this series: Joshua and Judges. I think it is difficult for Christians to reconcile the amount of bloodshed and battle contained in this section of the Bible with the golden-rule message of the New Testament.

But the fact is, God promised the land of Canaan to the Israelites. They left it to keep from starving and then ended up in slavery. While they were gone, other people, who worshiped other gods, moved in. God had to help them take it back.

I think it is important to embrace this part of our Christian history. For children, especially boys, it takes Sunday school firmly out of the realm of boring and into the action-packed world of awesome.

Just for fun, search the Internet for images of the judges in the Bible, so you can see how artists have depicted them over the years. I think you will be surprised.

PRAYER

Sometimes I think we need a reminder that God loves a passionate heart. While you pray, let's take two verses, one from the Old Testament and one from the New Testament, and embrace the God-given, fiery spirit within us.

OLD TESTMENT

> Have I not commanded you? Be strong and of good courage; be not frightened, neither be dismayed; for the LORD your God is with you wherever you go. (Joshua 1:9)

NEW TESTAMENT

> For God did not give us a spirit of timidity but a spirit of power and love and self-control. (2 Timothy 1:7)

MEMORY VERSE

> Have I not commanded you? Be strong and of good courage; be not frightened, neither be dismayed; for the LORD your God is with you wherever you go. (Joshua 1:9)

OBJECTIVES

1. Sing a historical story: "Joshua Fought the Battle of Jericho."
2. Connect the tribes of Israel on a Bible map to the twelve sons of Jacob and God's promise to Abraham.
3. Put the first eight books of the Bible in order.

ACTIVITIES

GOD'S GAME FACE

Prepare: Purchase eye black from a sports or general store. Eye black is a greasy combination of beeswax, paraffin, and carbon, which athletes use under their eyes to reduce the glare from the sun. Using eye black allows them to focus on the task at hand and let's face it, makes them look pretty tough too. Eye black can be removed using soap. You can also purchase stickers that look like eye black if you don't want to deal with the mess.

Explain: In the last lesson, we finished talking about the Law or the first five books of the Bible. In this lesson, we start a brand new section called the History. With the new section also comes a new memory verse. Let's focus and be ready to recite the new Bible verse by getting our game face on. This verse is our battle cry! Let's say it together.

Hint: This might be a tradition you will want to continue and repeat for the entire discussion of the History books.

JOSHUA FOUGHT THE BATTLE OF JERICHO! (AND OTHER BATTLE CRIES)

Prepare: This activity requires some singing. If you are uncomfortable singing the song yourself, find a tape of the song, "Joshua Fought the Battle of Jericho," find a friend who can sing it, or get a tablet and search for it on the Internet.

Explain: The first book of the History section is named after Joshua. Joshua was the next leader of Israel after Moses died. Joshua led the people of Israel back into the land of Canaan for the purpose of taking it over. The very first city he captured was Jericho. We are going to learn a song about that battle.

Ask: Why would a group of people want to build a wall around the city they live in? Are there examples of walled cities today?

Sing: "Joshua Fought the Battle of Jericho"

> Chorus: Joshua fought the battle of Jericho, Jericho, Jericho. Joshua fought the battle of Jericho and the walls came tumbling down.

> Verse 1: You may talk about your men of Gideon, you may talk about your men of Saul. But there's none like good old Joshua, and the battle of Jericho!

> (Chorus)

Verse 2: Right up to the walls of Jericho, they marched with spear in hand. "Go blow them ram horns," Joshua cried, "Cause the battle is in my hand."

(Chorus)

Verse 3: Then the lamb, ram sheep horns began to blow, and the trumpets began to sound. Joshua told the children to shout that morning and the walls came tumbling down!

(Chorus)

—African Spiritual, Public Domain

Tip: To make the story visual, show the children pictures of artists' renditions of the ancient city of Jericho.

Look it Up: The Twelve Tribes of Israel

Prepare: Write Genesis 17:1–8 on a whiteboard or where all the children can see it. Gather enough Bibles so each child has one. Find a map that shows the land of Canaan and outlines where each of the twelve tribes settled. Using the star template in the back of the book, make four stars for the star wall or chart with the names for this chapter: Joshua, Samson, Deborah, and Gideon.

Explain: Look up the Bible verses and read them together. When finished, find the map of Canaan that shows the twelve tribes of Israel.

By the time of Joshua, the descendants of the twelve brothers were all gathered into family groups called tribes. The tribes were named after the brother from which they were descended. For example, most scholars agree Joshua was from the tribe of Ephraim, which we know (see hint below) was one of the sons of Joseph.

Talk about how Joshua helped the tribes of Israel take back the land of Canaan and settle there. Each one of the tribes had its own piece of land. After the land was settled, there were leaders called Judges, who continued to fight and keep the territories safe from enemies. Some of the more famous judges were Samson, Deborah, and Gideon.

Scholars believe Samson was from the tribe of Dan. He was known for his inhuman strength. He once killed an entire Philistine army with the jawbone of a donkey (Judges 13:1–16: 21).

Experts feel Gideon was from the tribe of Joseph. He was a fearless military leader who destroyed temples of the foreign god Baal (Judges 6:1–25).

Some scholars place Deborah in the tribe of Issachar. She was a military leader who led an attack against the king of Canaan and his military general Sisera, which ended in the king's defeat (Judges 4:1–14).

Ask: What did God promise Abraham? How many of the promises came true? Who were the Israelites? Where were they at the end of the last lesson? What did God help Joshua do? Who remembers the names of the twelve sons of Jacob? Do you see any of those names on the map? Which of the twelve tribes were allowed to settle where Jerusalem is?

Hint: The twelve tribes of Israel are named after Jacob's twelve sons with two exceptions. Joseph had two boys named Ephraim and Manasseh. Both boys received their own area of Canaan to settle their families in. The tribe of Levi, because it was the tribe of priests and of Moses, split up. Some of them settled in each tribal land to help the entire Israelite family worship God properly.

When you talk about the Judges and Joshua, put their stars on the chart, lined up with the proper tribe. After explaining what a tribe is, check for understanding by asking the children what tribe they are from.

A note about tribes and Bible figures: There are as many theories about which tribe some biblical figures are from as there are scholars to explain it. The tribes I've suggested were found after researching various biblical sites and resources. Sometimes, though, it's a toss-up. Regardless, the important thing is to connect the historical figure to the family of Abraham. If you disagree with a tribe I've chosen, use your own research-based tribal ancestor.

The Book of Ruth: A History Mystery

Prepare: Make a star for Ruth using the template in the back of the book.

Explain: There is a third book we are covering in this lesson. It is the book of Ruth. The book of Ruth is a story about Ruth and Naomi. Naomi was an Israelite from the tribe of Judah. When her husband died, she decided to return to her home and family in Bethlehem. Ruth, wanting to make sure Naomi got there safely, insisted on going with Naomi on the journey. When they got to the land of Judah, Ruth married Naomi's kinsman Boaz.

Ask: Why is there a whole book in the Bible for a story about someone from the tribe of Judah? What else is special about the tribe of Judah? Have any of you ever wondered why this story of Abraham and his family is in the Bible?

Tips: In this activity, you are planting the idea that the story of Abraham ultimately leads to Jesus. When working on your star wall, somehow emphasize the stars representing Abraham, Isaac, Jacob, Judah, and all of the descendants of Judah with special markings that visually separate them from all the others. Don't answer the question in this lesson. Just let it hang there like a juicy piece of fruit on a branch adding an element of mystery to the lessons.

Prayer/Closing

Prepare: Place the memory verse in a place where everyone can see it.

Explain: Pray the Bible verse together old-school style. Begin by talking about the differences between the words *brave, strong, alarmed*, and *terrified*. We pray as a way of reminding ourselves that God is with us just like he was with Joshua so long ago. Have the kids bow their heads, clasp their hands, and sit quietly until it is time to repeat the verse together.

Ask: Which of the words in this verse are synonyms (the same)? Which ones are antonyms (different)? Which words is God commanding Joshua to be in this verse? Which words is God telling Joshua not to be? Why is God commanding Joshua to be brave and strong in the second half of the verse?

Pray:

> Leader: Dear God, Thank you for reminding Joshua that you are with him wherever he goes. Whenever we get alarmed and terrified, help us to remember your words to him.

> All: "Have I not commanded you? Be strong and of good courage; be not frightened, neither be dismayed; for the LORD your God is with you wherever you go." Amen. (Joshua 1:9)

Parent Connection

Take the Memory Verse Home

Was this a verse Paul was channeling when he wrote to the Ephesians about the armor of God? Joshua used his confidence in God's presence to conquer Canaan. Today, we don't have the Ark of the Covenant going before us to clear a path as we walk, but we can take Paul's advice and walk with God's armor on us.

Encourage the children to imagine putting on God's armor as they practice their memory verse while getting dressed each morning. Like Joshua, it is important to remember every day that God is with us wherever we go.

Tip: Christian bookstores often have Armor of God cards, bookmarks, or posters for children. These are great to purchase as a gift to send home following this lesson.

Chapter 7
Of Peace and Kings

Prepare

King David and King Solomon are, in my opinion, two of the coolest dude's in the Bible. These two men lived during a time of peace and prosperity for the Israelites. When King David and King Solomon were at the helm, Israel was in the zone!

First, there was King David—the musician. Handsome, athletic, and musically gifted, David was born to worship the Lord. Take your Bible, open it to the middle, and find Psalms. Whatever you are looking at was probably written by David. From his beginnings as a boy who was pretty good with a slingshot, to his cat and mouse games with Saul, and ending with his reign on the throne, David was *the man*.

Following right behind David, came his son, King Solomon. Known as the wise king, he is credited with writing both Ecclesiastes and the Song of Solomon. Under Solomon's rule, Israel grew into a kingdom of power and wealth. Stories about Solomon sparkle with opulence and splendor. Solomon used the Israelites' wealth to demonstrate to the world that God was worthy of being honored and worshiped with the very best money can buy.

Even though as Americans it is difficult to wrap our heads around the concept of a king, we do understand the power of strong, charismatic, and wise leadership. People love to follow a competent leader. David and Solomon demonstrated that behind strong leadership, there is the hand and will of God. By putting God first in their lives, David, Solomon, and the Israelites prospered.

As you prepare, just for fun, search for the phrase Solomon's Temple in your web browser. You'll find terrific images and diagrams of what it might have looked like, which have been lifted from the pages of the Bible by artists. Artists have a way of making words jump off a page and burn into our memories.

We can read about the fabulous furnishings and colors of Solomon's Temple and attempt to create them on our own, or we can look at pictures and realize it was one fancy place! One artist reminds us the building itself was no bigger than a tennis court. But, as we all know, it's not what was on the outside but what was on the inside that counted.

This lesson is all about celebrating God's accomplishment of fulfilling a promise to Abraham. God made Abraham's descendants into a great nation of people called the Israelites. He sent Joshua and the judges into the land of Canaan and conquered it so Abraham's family would have a beautiful slice of earth to call home. He gave them King David and King Solomon so they could enjoy years of peace and prosperity. God is indeed good, and God does keep his promises.

Prayer

God, thank you for believing in humans enough to raise them to levels even they don't think they can reach. Thank you for not giving up on us. Thank you for always believing we will do the right thing and be our best selves. Help us to continue to honor you with our time, our talents, and our treasures. Help us to always celebrate you, what you have done for us, and what you do through and with us.

Memory Verse

Have I not commanded you? Be strong and of good courage; be not frightened, neither be dismayed; for the LORD your God is with you wherever you go. (Joshua 1:9)

Objectives

1. Meet King David, the musician.
2. Meet King Solomon, the wise man.
3. Build Solomon's Temple.

Activities

Decorate a Crown

Prepare: Cut out the crown pattern and use it to trace a crown on a large piece of construction paper. Make sure the paper you use is large enough to make crowns that will fit around the each child's head.

Let the children cut out the traced crown, making sure it is long enough to go around their heads. Give the children markers, crayons, sequins, and stickers to decorate their crowns. Help the children adjust their crowns to fit their heads.

Tip: Do it yourself (DIY) crowns are available at party supply stores for a small amount of money. They are typically available for purchase in packages of twelve.

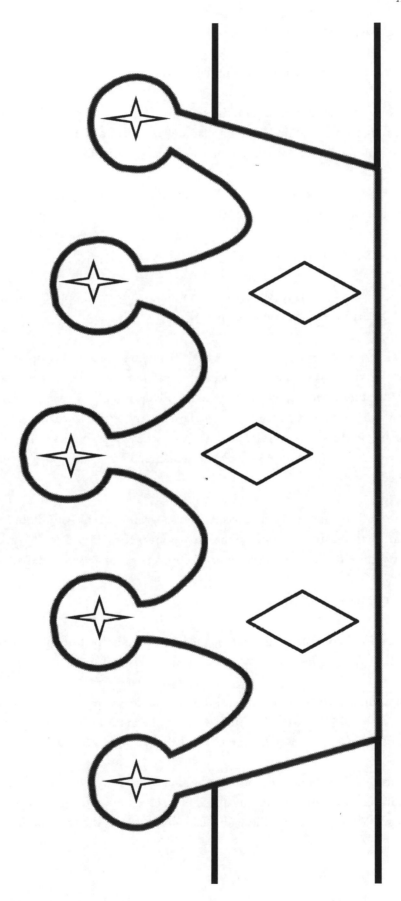

MEET SAMUEL, THE PROPHET/JUDGE

Prepare: Make a star for Samuel using the template in the back of the book.

Explain: In the last lesson, we talked about Judges. Scholars say Samuel was considered to be the last judge. He was also known as the first prophet. Samuel went to help the priests when he was very young. God called Samuel into service when he was twelve years old (1 Samuel 3:1–21).

Hint: Samuel was from the tribe of Levi. Spend a little time comparing Samuel's age to the children in your class. If you have time to read the story, the verses are extremely accessible for children.

MEET KING DAVID, THE MUSICIAN

Prepare: Make a star for David using the template in the back of the book. If you are using a living history figure, make arrangements for your special guest's visit.

Explain: After Canaan was firmly in the hands of the Israelites, kings were appointed to rule over the land. Two of the kings were the most successful and famous. The first one was King David. David is known, by most people, as the boy who killed Goliath with a slingshot and a stone (1 Samuel 17). David grew up to be handsome and famous and was a musician. He is credited with writing many of the Psalms. "Amazing Grace," a well-known gospel hymn, is said to be based on David's prayer in 1 Chronicles 17:16–17. David worshiped the Lord and was astonished by his blessings and grace.

Tip: While you are talking about David, place David's star in the tribe of Judah. If you have time, recruit someone from the church to come to the classroom as King David and to talk to the children as a living history figure. If not, search the Internet for pictures of David and discuss his story.

MEET KING SOLOMON: THE WISE MAN

Prepare: Make a star for Solomon using the template in the back of the book. If you are using a living history figure, make arrangements for your special guest's visit.

Explain: King Solomon was the second famous king in Israelite history. Solomon was wise. He asked God for wisdom to rule the throne (2 Chronicles 1:1–12). The most famous story about him was how he settled an argument between two women over a baby (1 Kings 3:16–28).

Tips: If you have time, recruit someone from the church to appear in the classroom as King Solomon and talk to the children as a living history figure. If not, search the Internet for pictures of Solomon and discuss his story. Place his star on the wall beside his father in the tribe of Judah.

BUILD SOLOMON'S TEMPLE

Prepare: Print a copy of the temple diagram at the end of this activity. Gather blocks or other building materials. Find yellow construction paper to decorate the temple and make the Ark of the Covenant. Gather felt or some other heavy material to make the temple curtain.

Explain: Solomon is most famous for building the first permanent temple for God. Prior to this time, the temple was made of tents and was called the Tabernacle. It traveled with the Israelites and was with them as they fought to reclaim the Promised Land (2 Chronicles 2:1–10). Point out the parts of the temple and how they were used. Build the basic outline of the temple out of your prepared building materials and using the diagram.

Ask: Who could go inside the temple? Who could go inside the Holy of Holies? What was the purpose of animal sacrifices for? Who did people rely on to help them talk to God? Do you think people felt like they could talk to God directly? Who could talk to God directly?

Hint: To make this lesson more visual, search the Internet or find a picture of an artist's rendition of the temple for the children to look at. There are several great cutaways showing the temple in all of its glory.

Point out the parts of the temple and how they were used. The point in this lesson is to allow the children to study the temple and its parts in great detail. What you create does not have to be perfect or even beautiful.

This is an excellent time to discuss that the only people allowed inside the temple were priests. The only person who could enter the Holy of Holies and God's presence was the high priest, and this happened only once a year. Jewish men were allowed to stand on the temple porch. Jewish women were allowed to come into the temple courtyard. Gentiles were not allowed within the temple grounds.

Solomon's Temple

Inner Court

Alter

Molten Sea
(for washing)

Porch

Holy Place

Storage Rooms

Storage Rooms

Outer Court

Inner Court

Holy of Holies

Ark

Storage Rooms

Prayer/Closing

Prepare: Write 1 Chronicles 17:16–17 (David's Prayer).

Explain: Look up the passage in the Bible and read the words that David prayed to God together. Then sing or play the first verse of "Amazing Grace."

> Amazing grace, how sweet the sound, that saved a wretch like me. I once was lost, but now am found, was blind but now I see.—John Newton (1725–1807)

Parent Connection

Take the Memory Verse Home

King David and King Solomon knew how to live supported by God. Their fearless leadership gave the Israelites a lengthy period of wealth, peace, and prosperity. In this lesson, we are focusing on the section that tells us not to be "afraid or terrified."

Discuss things children do that scare them (cleaning a toilet or sink, walking to their beds in the dark, sleeping without night-lights, eating vegetables they don't like). Challenge them, while they are at home, to do one of the things that scares them as they repeat the memory verse.

Chapter 8
United We Stand, Divided We Fall

Prepare

There's only one way to separate yourself from God, and that's if *you* do it. Even then, you aren't really separated from him. You are simply ignoring his hands reaching out to help.

The next chapter in the history of Israel is unfortunately not as happy as the time of King David and King Solomon. History and the Bible teach us that, sometimes, the very wealth and prosperity that were enjoyed in King Solomon's reign were the beginning of Israel's undoing.

When people choose to separate themselves from God, priorities get offtrack. This was certainly the case for the Israelites. Not only did their kingdom split in two, but one leader of the northern kingdom of Israel (King Ahab) actually let his wife convince him he should worship Baal instead of God.

I wonder how God feels when he sees his people—the people he has protected and given so much to—turning from him seemingly without a thought or a care. I can feel his sadness. I can feel his pain. Yet we do it all the time. We turn from him because we are weak. We turn from him because our egos get in the way. We start to think we are in control. We begin to think we are more powerful than God is.

But the good news is that God gives us chances to change. Even though King Ahab went off the deep end, God sent him Elijah. In one of the more colorful passages in the Bible, Ahab and Elijah face off to see which god is more powerful. When it's all over, it is very clear who is following the right path and who is kidding himself.

There is nothing like public embarrassment to set things straight. But it seems humans have very short memories. Over and over again, the Israelites strayed from God and his protection. Over and over again, they had to learn lessons the hard way. Ultimately, they ended up losing the very land God fought so hard to get them.

So how do we do it? How do we keep God in our lives? Like any relationship, we have to work at it. Think about how you connect with your friends and family. You eat dinner with them on a daily basis. You have conversations with them several times a day. You text them. You make appointments to go and do things together.

Is Sunday morning the only time you make an appointment to hang out with God? How many times do you decide you're really too tired to even do that? It's time to challenge ourselves to spend more time with God.

When God is first in our lives, and we spend regular, daily time with him, our priorities are in the right place. When we let God in, he works on us. When we let God in, he blesses us. When we let God in, he gives us peace.

Before this lesson, go back and revisit David's prayer: 1 Chronicles 17:16–17. Then spend some time on YouTube listening to versions of the song "Amazing Grace," which is based on this prayer.

> A couple of my favorites are found at:
> http://www.youtube.com/watch?v=wqG8TOPwzIA
> http://www.youtube.com/watch?v=jyM9sRqR9Uk

MEMORY VERSE

> Have I not commanded you? Be strong and of good courage; be not frightened, neither be dismayed; for the LORD your God is with you wherever you go. (Joshua 1:9)

OBJECTIVES

1. Find the northern kingdom of Israel and the southern kingdom of Judah on a map.
2. Find Assyria and Babylonia on a map.
3. Act out the story of King Ahab and Elijah.

ACTIVITIES

MAP IT: THE DIVIDED KINGDOM

Prepare: Find a map in a Bible or a Bible atlas that shows the northern and southern kingdoms of Israel.

Explain: After Solomon's death, the Israelites who lived in the north began to fight with the Israelites who lived in Jerusalem and in the south. They fought about how they should worship God and whether or not they should also worship other gods. Eventually, they fought so much that they ended up splitting into two kingdoms with two separate kings. There was a northern kingdom and a southern kingdom. The northern kingdom separated from God first. Then the southern kingdom separated from God as well.

Ask: Who can find the northern kingdom on your map? Who can find the southern kingdom? Where is Jerusalem? Do you think God was happy or sad that the Israelites were choosing to worship other gods?

Hint: The two kingdoms were Israel (the north) and Judah (the south).

Look It Up: King Ahab Versus Elijah

Prepare: Prepare to act out the King Ahab versus Elijah showdown with whatever props you need. Write 1 Kings 18:22–39 on a whiteboard or piece of paper located where the children can all see it. Make one star for Ahab and one for Elijah using the template in the back of the book. Using another piece of colorful paper, write the word "versus" to hang between the stars.

Explain: In the last lesson, we learned about two of the greatest rulers the Israelites ever had. In this lesson, we will learn about one of their worst kings—King Ahab. King Ahab was the ruler of the northern kingdom. God was upset with him because King Ahab told his people to worship the pagan god Baal. God sent the prophet Elijah to correct Ahab's wrongdoing.

Look up the 1 Kings Bible passage and read it together. Act out the standoff between God and Baal using the Bible story as your script.

Ask: What did Elijah propose was the best way to test who was the real god? Did the priests of Baal succeed in calling fire down on the sacrifice? What did Elijah do to his sacrifice that would have made it impossible to burn? Did Elijah's sacrifice burn? Which god was the real god?

Hint: Elijah is thought to be from the tribe of Gad, and Ahab is thought to be from the tribe of Ephraim (one of Joseph's sons).

Tip: Read the story in advance and plan what the children act out. The key is simplicity. Two tables placed strategically in a room can be altars. Stuffed animals can be sacrifices. Pretend to use buckets and shovels to dig trenches and pour water. The important thing is to allow the children to use their bodies to reenact this classic showdown.

Foreign Armies

Prepare: Find a map that shows the lands of Assyria and Babylonia on it. Find a modern-day map or globe of the same area. Place the temple you created in the last lesson nearby.

Explain: Elijah's win worked for a while, but the people continued to separate themselves from God. So God sent more prophets like Elijah to warn the Israelites that foreign armies would come and conquer Canaan. Sometimes the warnings worked and the people would repent. Eventually, however, foreign armies came, as predicted, and took the land of Canaan away from the Israelites.

Assyria conquered the northern kingdom of Israel first. The Babylonian army conquered both the Assyrians and the southern kingdom of Judah. The Babylonians removed the Israelite people from Canaan and made them slaves. In the process, they looted and destroyed the temple.

When finished, show the children the chart of the kings of Israel and discuss the fickle nature of rulers over time.

Tip: Find the countries of Assyria and Babylonia on a map to make the story visual. If you have a tablet or can getthe Internet on your phone, search for pictures of the area to show what it looks like today. Pretend you are Babylonians and loot and destroy the temple you built during the last lesson (Don't worry, you will rebuild it in the next lesson). Leave the pieces on the table.

KINGS OF ISRAEL

UNITED KINGDOM	
KING SAUL	STARTED GOOD, WENT BAD
KING DAVID	GOOD
KING SOLOMON	MOSTLY GOOD

DIVIDED KINGDOM			
ISRAEL		JUDAH	
JEROBOAM I	BAD	REHOBOAM	GOOD, THEN BAD
NADAB	BAD	ABIJAH	BAD
BAASHA	BAD	ASA	GOOD, THEN BAD
ELAH	BAD	JEHOSHAPHAT	GOOD
ZIMRI	BAD	JEHORAM	BAD
TIBNI	BAD	AHAZIAH	BAD
OMRI	BAD	QUEEN ATHALIAH	BAD
AHAB	BAD	JOASH	GOOD, THEN BAD
AHAZIAH	BAD	AMAZIAH	MOSTLY GOOD
JORAM	BAD	UZZIAH	GOOD
JEHU	BAD	JOTHAM	GOOD
JEHOAHAZ	BAD	AHAZ	BAD
JEHOASH	BAD	HEZEKIAH	GOOD
JEROBOAM II	BAD	MANASSEH	BAD, THEN GOOD
ZECHARIAH	BAD	AMON	BAD
SHALLUM	BAD	JOSIAH	GOOD
MENAHEM	BAD	JEHOAHAZ	BAD
PEKAHIAH	BAD	JEHOIAKIM	BAD
PEKAH	BAD	JEHOIACHIN	BAD
HOSHEA	BAD	ZEDEKIAH	BAD

*Information regarding Kings from Rose Book of Bible Charts, Maps and Timelines, Rose Publishing, Torrence, California, 2005

PRAYER/CLOSING

Prepare: Write the memory verse on a whiteboard, chalkboard, or flip chart where it can be easily seen.

Explain: An echo prayer is when the leader says one sentence and then the congregation repeats what the leader says. Say the prayer together.

> Leader: Lord, you've commanded us to be brave and strong.
> Children: Lord, you've commanded us to be brave and strong.
>
> Leader: Lord, you've told us not to be alarmed or terrified.
> Children: Lord, you've told us not to be alarmed or terrified.
>
> Leader: Why, Lord? Why are we to remember to be these things?
> Children: Why, Lord? Why are we to remember to be these things?
>
> Leader: Because you have promised to be with us wherever we go.
> Children: Because you have promised to be with us wherever we go.

PARENT CONNECTION

TAKE THE MEMORY VERSE HOME

Prepare: Print one or two common table prayers on a business card template for the children to take home.

Explain: A very simple way to remind yourself daily to follow God is to implement a prayer before meal times. Ask your family to pray before each meal.

Tip: Two common table prayers are:

> God is great. God is good. Let us thank him for our food.
> Come, Lord Jesus, be our guest. Let these gifts to us be blessed.

CROSS IN YOUR POCKET

Another way to always remember that God is with you is to carry a cross in your pocket. These small, metallic crosses can be purchased at Christian bookstores. As an alternative, small wooden crosses can be found or made and used.

CHAPTER 9

I GET KNOCKED DOWN, BUT I GET UP AGAIN

PREPARE

Over and over again, God sends salvation in the oddest times and through the oddest circumstances. In the history, salvation came in the form of King Cyrus of Persia. That's right, Persia. Take a trip in your mind to the stories of the Arabian Nights. My mind instantly fills with images of colorful, cloth flowing around beautiful palaces and people.

Cyrus the Great of Persia is known for accomplishing great things. Scholars tell us he chose and followed a well-documented policy of religious tolerance during his rule, which allowed minority religions to worship and practice religion as they saw fit. After conquering the Babylonians, he allowed the exiled Israelites to return to their homeland of Canaan and rebuild Solomon's Temple in Jerusalem. He also returned many of the artifacts, which had been stolen from inside the temple, to the Jews.

Purged of their idol worship, the Israelites returned to their homeland, not as rulers but as residents. In Ezra, the Jewish people rebuilt Solomon's Temple. Nehemiah recounts the rebuilding of the wall that protected Jerusalem. Esther became Queen of Persia and ended up saving the Jews who decided to stay behind. After years of division and destruction, healing and salvation came. God is an awesome God.

In this lesson, we are again reminded God is never far away. The world knocks us down in many ways, but God is always there to build us back up. Most of the time, God appears in ways that are unexpected and unforeseen. We just have to wait, never lose hope, and keep looking for God's hand in our lives and the events arounds us. In short, it's our job to keep the faith.

As you prepare this lesson, look back on the events in your life and search for God's hand in them. Is there a time where you can see God leading you in a certain direction? Is there an event that initially seemed not so great but eventually led you to something terrific? How much do you trust that God is with you all the time? How much do you trust God that will always be there for you no matter what happens in your life?

If you have time, rent and watch *One Night with the King*, It is the 2006 story of Esther directed by Michael O. Sajbel. It's a beautiful depiction of the Persian Empire and the book of Esther.

Prayer

God, I know you are always with me. I have seen your work in my life, and I can tell you have been involved in directing my path. Sometimes when life is challenging and things aren't going my way, it is easy to lose sight of the fact you are there. Help me in those times to remember the stories of Ezra, Nehemiah, and Esther. Help me to remember their faith in you. Give me the faith to hold on, to hope, and to wait patiently for salvation.

Memory Verse

Have I not commanded you? Be strong and of good courage; be not frightened, neither be dismayed; for the LORD your God is with you wherever you go. (Joshua 1:9)

Objectives

1. Find Persia on a map.
2. Rebuild Solomon's Temple
3. Put the first seventeen books of the Bible in order.

Activities

Look It Up: Who Was King Cyrus?

Prepare: Write the Bible passage of Ezra 1:1–11 on a whiteboard or a piece of paper and place it where every child can see it.

Explain: Look up the Bible passage and read it together.

Ask: Who gave King Cyrus the idea to let the Jews rebuild the temple? What did people do to help rebuild the temple? How many articles of gold and silver did King Cyrus find in the treasury of the Babylonian King Nebuchadnezzar? What were some of the things recorded in the inventory? Was King Cyrus a good man?

Map It: Queen Esther

Prepare: Find a map showing the Persian Empire. Also find a map showing the area today. Make a star for Esther using the template in the back of the book.

Explain: King Cyrus of Persia beat the Babylonians and freed the Israelite slaves. Any of the Israelites who wanted to go back home to the land of Canaan were allowed to go. Some returned, and some stayed behind in Persia. Esther is the last book of the History section of the Bible and is also the name of a person who stayed behind in Persia. Esther is the story of a Jewish woman who became the queen of Persia.

Ask: How big was the Persian Empire? Is Canaan still part of the Persian Empire? When the Israelites were allowed to go back to their homeland, do you think their land had stayed the same or was it now different?

Solomon's Temple and Walls Rebuilt

Prepare: Create one star for Ezra and one for Nehemiah using the template at the back of the book. Get the temple diagram from the last lesson and have it nearby for the reconstruction.

Explain: Ezra and Nehemiah are two books about people who, when freed by King Cyrus, decided to return to Jerusalem. Ezra was responsible for rebuilding Solomon's Temple. Ezra and the Israelites weren't able to rebuild the temple exactly as it had been before, but it still felt good to rebuild God's house and have a place where they could worship him. Nehemiah rebuilt the walls around Jerusalem so the Israelites, who had returned, would be safe.

Using the building materials from the temple you destroyed in the last lesson, rebuild the basic outline of the temple using the temple diagram from the last lesson.

Ask: Have you ever known anyone who lost his or her home to a fire, flood, or other natural disaster? How would it feel to lose everything you have? How good would it feel to be given the opportunity to build it again? What was different about this new temple? Was it the same as when it had originally been built by Solomon?

Hint: When you rebuild something, inevitably, it will be different than it was before. This is okay. Here is a good opportunity to explain how an experience can sometimes change who we are. The change doesn't have to be labeled good or bad. It's just different.

Prayer/Closing

Prepare: Place the memory verse where the children can see it. Divide the class into two groups or have a leader ask the questions and the children answer them.

Explain: This prayer is called an "Ask and Repeat" prayer. This prayer is meant to be said with gusto! Read the question and the proper response until the children understand what to do and then say the prayer together.

> Group #1: What does the LORD ask of you?
> Group #2: To be brave and strong!

Group #2: Where is the LORD?

Group #1: With us wherever we go!

PARENT CONNECTION

By now, the children should have seventeen books of the Bible and two memory verses memorized. Challenge them to show off their newly acquired knowledge by naming them in order for a family member or arrange to show off the children's skills in an adult Sunday school class or in front of the church congregation. Recite the memorized Bible verses and books of the Bible. You may want to practice with them to prepare. Show the adults how you learn by playing some of your favorite Bible memory games with them.

CHAPTER 10

WHEN IT RAINS, IT POURS

PREPARE

The jury is out on reruns. Are you a fan? Are you not a fan? I like watching reruns of my favorite shows. I'm also one of those people who will purchase a favorite book or movie so I can relive the story over and over. I refuse to count the number of times I have seen or read anything by Jane Austin.

The next sections of the Bible are a little bit like reruns. In the History section (Judges through Esther), we learned all about the chronological story of the Israelite people after they conquered Canaan, which was a period of time that covered about one thousand years. One thousand years is ten generations. That's the difference between today and the early 1900s. In the 1900s, silent movies were just beginning to be shown, Einstein proposed his theory of relativity for the first time, plastic was invented, and our first efforts to reach the North Pole were realized.

One thousand years is a lot of territory for twelve books. We covered it all in four lessons—definitely only hit the highlights. So the great thing about discovering the Bible is that we get to go back and do some reruns. Imagine flying over this timeline at one hundred thousand feet in your cape and superhero gear. Then imagine flying back over the timeline and using your powerful eyesight to focus in on bits and parts of it to learn more details. That is what we are about to do.

Where do we start? Let's start in my *favorite* section of the Bible—the Poetry and Wisdom Literature. Here, the creative talent of the judges and the kings of that period is on display.

The book we will start with is Job. Job was doomed from the very beginning. His name means "persecuted" in Hebrew. As you can imagine, Job is not a popular baby name. It doesn't even break the top one thousand, but what a story. It has drama. It has deep emotion and suffering. Best of all, it has a happy ending. What is the purpose of the story? The story of Job demonstrates patience under persecution. It glorifies the all-powerful nature of God. It has much to say about remaining faithful, even when your world is upside down.

The story of Job also allows us to examine the next step in the production of the written word. The oldest versions of the Old Testament were discovered written on stone and clay tablets. This period of one thousand years was one of peace as well as amazing growth for the Israelite nation. Thank you, God, for this period of creativity and inspiration, which produced the written word. Because of these years, we can read today what was on the minds of your people so long ago.

PRAYER AND MEDITATION

To prepare for this lesson, watch an amazing YouTube video of the child preacher Samuel Green as he tells his favorite Bible story—the story of Job. Samuel's version of the story is abridged. But while you watch, say a prayer of thanks to God for children who seem to get things a little better and a little quicker than adults do.

http://www.youtube.com/watch?v=LpWe1XuhvRU

MEMORY VERSE

> Trust in the LORD with all your heart, and do not rely on your own insight. In all your ways acknowledge him, and he will make straight your paths. (Proverbs 3:5–6)

OBJECTIVES

1. Write on a clay tablet.
2. Discover and read the introduction to the book of Job.
3. Put the first eighteen books of the Bible in order.

ACTIVITIES

WRITE A MESSAGE IN CLAY

Prepare: Gather modeling clay and toothpicks.

Explain: Flatten your modeling clay on the table into a square or rectangular shape. Using the toothpick, have each child write his or her name or something else of that child's choice into the clay. Make sure the word is written deep enough and big enough to be read when the clay dries.

Tips: Use modeling clay that isn't reusable. It should dry into a permanent, stonelike sculpture. Send the clay piece home to finish drying or let it dry overnight in the classroom to be taken home the next time the class meets.

EARLY CLAY TABLETS

Prepare: With a tablet or your phone, search images of early stone and clay tablets showing cuneiform writing.

Explain: In earlier lessons, we learned that the stories of the Bible were passed down from generation to generation like stories around a campfire. Some of the first forms of writing were on clay tablets using cuneiform characters. Writing details in the Bible down made them more permanent, but the technology of clay didn't come without its problems. Clay tablets were heavy and broke easily. As a result, they were often kept very small.

Ask: What were the advantages of writing Bible stories on stone and clay tablets? What were the disadvantages of writing the Bible stories on stone and clay tablets?

Hint: Cuneiform is pronounced "KYOO-nee-form."

Look It Up: The Story of Job

Prepare: Gather one Bible for each child—preferably a Bible that contains a child-friendly introduction to each book of the Bible.

Explain: In some Bibles, the books have an introduction that explains what the book is about. Study Bibles have introductions that have other important information as well. Find the book of Job. Read and explore the introduction materials together.

Ask: Based on what we have read, what do you think the book of Job is about? What is the message of Job's writer? Does the introduction make you want to read the book? Why or why not? What other introductions do you want to explore?

Hint: This is typically a brand-new discovery for most children. After reading the introduction to Job, they will potentially be interested in reading more. Let their curiosity and the clock guide your time together.

Tip: Another popular Bible commonly given to children is called the Action Bible. The Action Bible is a graphic version of the Bible stories written and edited by Doug Mauss and illustrated by Sergio Cariello. If you can, access a copy of this Bible to show to the children. Discuss how Bibles such as these serve as introductions to the stories in the books of the Bible. Find the story of Job and look at it together.

Trust Fall

Prepare: Find a large, empty space that is free of obstacles that might cause problems. Ideally, find a room, such as a gymnasium, with a soft mat on the floor.

Explain: The book of Job is about trusting God. Job put his complete faith and trust in God even though his life became challenging. The author of Job is telling us that no one knows our part in God's plan but God. Trusting totally in someone else is difficult. Let's do an experiment to see how willing you are to trust someone.

Trust Fall: In this exercise, one person is the catcher and one person is the faller. One at a time, have the faller stand with his or her back to the catcher. The faller should cross his or her arms over his or her chest, lock his or her knees, and fall backward into the catcher's arms. Start with a short space in between so the fall isn't far down. Widen the space for scarier falls.

Ask: Was trusting someone to catch you easy or hard? What did it feel like to fall backward? Do you think this is how Job felt when everything bad was happening to him? How is trusting God like falling backward?

Tips: If you have younger children, you will need to serve as the catcher in this exercise to provide for everyone's safety.

Telling a Story of Trust

Prepare: Write the word "Job" on a colorful piece of paper. If you are feeling creative, decorate the paper to look like a tiny book. If you are not, making something look like a book is as simple as cutting a rectangle out of a brown piece of paper.

Explain: The book of Job is a story told by the Israelites, throughout their early history, as an object lesson for trusting God no matter what. Scholars are unsure of who wrote Job or when or even if the story actually happened, but the story was part of the Dead Sea Scrolls, so they know it has been around for a long time. It is impossible to tell if Job was a real person and even more difficult to tell where he fit in the Israelite family. What we do know is that the story was commonly told.

Tip: Place the book of Job on the star wall in the general area of the History characters to represent a story that is common to all the Israelites.

Why Do Bad Things Happen?

The story of Job sometimes brings up questions about why bad things happen to good people. If this issue arises as you discuss the story, don't ignore it. It's okay to question God, to argue with him, to be angry with him. God already knows what is on your heart. Being honest about what is there isn't disrespectful. Being honest about what is on your heart helps God lead you to answers. In the story, Job became angry with God. Job prayed and asked God why these bad things were happening to him (Job 9:25–10:22).

Unfortunately, evil exists in the world that God cannot control. Evil causes people to make bad choices and to do bad things. God can't always stop evil things from happening because we don't live in a perfect world. What we can trust is that God will always do his best to help us through the bad situations that come our way. Ultimately, in the end of days, God's ways will win (Job 36–37).

Meanwhile, only God knows what is best for us. When we pray to God, we must remember God will help us in a way He feels is best. It's our job to trust him. Like Job, we need to respect God's authority and trust in his plan for our lives (Job 42).

Prayer/Closing

Prepare: Make sure the memory verse is located where the children can see it.

Explain: Sometimes, words aren't necessary or needed when we pray. Sometimes, demonstrating our faith in God with our whole body is an appropriate way to pray. Let's pray with our whole body.

As the children do one final trust fall, have them say, "I trust you, God!" as they fall.

Parent Connection

Take the Memory Verse Home

Prepare: Print one copy of the Bible verse sign for each child.

Explain: Take this sign home to color and hang on the rearview mirror of the family car or the doorknob you use to exit the house. Before you exit the house or car, recite the memory verse to remind yourself that God has your back each and every day. If we trust in him and follow his lead, he will help us make good choices in life.

Chapter 11

Sing to the Lord

Prepare

Do you know that many songs have lyrics? The answer to that question is so simple and obvious. Yes. Some songs have lyrics. Everybody knows that. Songs are, after all, lyrics put to melody and rhythm. Sometimes, however, it is easy to get caught up in the music and the rhythm and to forget each one has a point or a message. We get so focused on melodies that we sing words and forget to think about what they mean. Psalms is a book of lyrics. The melodies and rhythms that once carried the words of the psalms are gone. The lyrics or the meaning of the psalms remain.

Lyrics are a form of poetry. Poetry is different. Poetry is special. Unlike prose, poetry is designed to elicit an emotional response. A poet writes to describe as opposed to writing to explain. The sound of the words becomes important. The images and feelings the phrases evoke in your mind take precedence over their meanings. The point of poetry is emotion. The point of poetry is feeling.

When a skilled musician takes highly charged words and puts them to music, they take on a life of their own. They become inspirational. They can send humans to places they cannot go by simply reading the words. In short, the book of Psalms is an extremely powerful place to visit.

Most of the psalms we read today are there because of King David and his choir director Asaph. The book is a collection of songs that the early Israelites used to worship the Lord. Some of them are happy. Some of them are sad. All of them describe the human experience and our relationship with God.

The lyrics in this book still inspire songwriters today. Look in the back of any church hymnal for the index of scripture references. Psalms is usually one of the biggest sections. The songs you will find are good songs:

> "O Lord How Majestic is Thy Name"
> "He Leadeth Me"
> "A Mighty Fortress Is Our God"
> "O God Our Help in Ages Past"
> "Joy to the World"

"Awesome God"
"Blessed Be Your Name"
"10,000 Reasons"

And the list goes on.

To prepare, spend some time with two of David's inspiring psalms: Psalm 8 and Psalm 63. As you read, think about the texture of the words. Read them aloud. How do the words sound coming out of your mouth? What images do the words inspire in your mind? What feelings do the words generate in your body? Take time to immerse yourself in the lyrical experience of worship.

If you need help feeling the emotion of these psalms, below are a couple of singers who get it right.

"How Majestic Is Your Name," by Amy Grant, found at:
http://www.youtube.com/watch?v=HCkEkueBPtc
"10,000 Reasons," by Matt Redman, found at:
http://www.youtube.com/watch?v=XtwIT8JjddM

PRAYER

Pick a psalm, any psalm. Read it aloud. Enjoy it. Pray it. Speak it to God. Here are some psalms of praise and thanksgiving: Psalm 92, 95, 103, 107, 116, 117, 118, 146, 147, 148, 149, 150.

MEMORY VERSE

Trust in the LORD with all your heart, and do not rely on your own insight. In all your ways acknowledge him, and he will make straight your paths. (Proverbs 3:5–6)

OBJECTIVES

1. Read a psalm written by David.
2. Discover how many songs in a church hymnal reference the book of Psalms.
3. Play a game using the first nineteen books of the Bible.

ACTIVITIES

MY FAVORITE WORSHIP SONG

Prepare: Find Christian music and something to play it on.

Explain: As the children arrive, have the music playing. Take requests and play favorites. Sing songs together. Include songs like "This Little Light of Mine," "Joshua Fought the Battle of Jericho," "Jesus Loves Me," and other children's songs.

Tips: CDs of worship songs can be purchased from Christian bookstores. Ask your church librarian if your church has a collection of Christian records or CDs. Your church music director may also be of help to you. You can always use an Internet radio station and stream contemporary Christian music or use YouTube to find specific songs you want to hear.

Make a Straw Panpipe

Prepare: Gather sixteen straws per child, some scissors, and colorful duct tape.

Explain: Have each child select sixteen straws and line them up evenly in a row. Very carefully, tape the straws together using a strip of duct tape. Tape the straws approximately one inch from one of the straw's ends. It is important as you are taping to keep the straws flat, even, and close together. On the opposite end from the duct tape, leave the two straws on one edge at their original length. Using the scissors, cut the next two straws approximately one inch shorter than the original straws. Continue until each pair of straws is cut shorter than the ones before them. Practice playing the panpipe by blowing into the straws at the even end.

Tip: Found in any general store or hardware store, a roll of duct tape can unleash a world of creativity. Because of this, duct tape now comes in an array of designs and colors. Let your imagination go wild.

Look It Up: The Psalms of David

Prepare: Write the Bible passages of Psalm 8 and Psalm 23 on a white-board or a piece of paper and place it where every child can see it.

Explain: Divide the children into two groups. Half of the children must find Psalm 8 in their Bibles. The other half should find Psalm 23.

The book of Psalms contains lyrics that David wrote and sang to God. It has songs written by other people as well. The people of Israel put the words to music and sang them when they worshipped God.

Read Psalm 8 and 23 as a group.

Ask: Who wrote these psalms? Who do you think the Bible is referring to? What do we remember about King David from our previous lessons?

Tips: On the star wall, have the children find King David and place a panpipe beside his name. Tape a piece of paper that says "Psalms" or write the word "Psalms" there.

Full of Psalms

Prepare: Gather your church hymnals or songbooks. Ensure these books have an index of scripture references in the back and/or list the scripture reference for the tune near the song title.

Explain: The songs we sing in church typically are written because the songwriter was inspired by a Bible verse or a passage. Find the index of scripture references and discover how many of the songs in the hymnbook were written or inspired by the psalms. Look particularly for songs written about Psalm 8 and 23. Sing one together.

Tips: Typically, the songs in church hymnals or songbooks are organized in an index by scripture reference to assist worship planners and pastors in choosing an appropriate song for the sermon topic. If you don't have access to such a book, ask your church musical director for suggestions or books he or she uses to plan the worship time.

Why Do We Sing?

Prepare: Invite your church organist, pianist, choir director, or music director to come to your classroom. Prepare that person for the experience by telling him or her the list of questions that individual will be asked.

Explain: Today we are going to have our guest explain to us why we sing in church and how the songs we sing are chosen.

Ask: How do you choose the songs for the church service? How do you find songs that match the theme of the sermon or the scripture being read? How important is singing during church? What do you think is the most important thing about being a church musician? What is your favorite part of the church service?

Tips: Children often have no idea that the songs sung during worship time have a purpose and are used to enhance the worship experience. Inviting the worship leaders in to talk with them closes this gap.

Prayer/Closing

Prepare: Display the memory verse where children can see it.

Explain: Singing is one of the best forms of praying. God enjoyed David's singing, and God enjoys hearing us sing as well. We should always make sure the words we are saying are pleasing to God.

Have the children stand in a circle and sing a closing prayer.

Prayer

Choose a song your children know well and sing it together ("Kum Ba Yah," "Jesus Loves Me," or "This Little Light of Mine"). As an alternative, play one of the group's favorite songs and listen or sing to the music.

Parent Connection

Take the Memory Verse Home

One way to "know God in all your paths," is to use age as a way to study the psalms. Challenge the children to find out the age of each member of their families. Then tell them to use their Bibles to read the psalm that is the same number as the age of each family member.

Chapter 12

The Wisdom of Kings

Prepare

Wisdom. There is an elusive word. What exactly does it mean anyway? Who has it? Do you have to be old to have it? My image of a wise person is the wizard Gandalf from *The Lord of the Rings* trilogy—or at least someone who looks like Gandalf. So, to me, being wise is having a flowing white beard, long white hair, and proper-looking wizard robes, right?

But as I consider my archetype of wisdom further, I think there is more than just the way he looks that makes me feel Gandalf is wise. It's also about what he says (with the help of author J. R. R. Tolkien, of course). Consider the following (my apologies to those who are unfamiliar with the books):

> Many that live deserve death. And some that die deserve life. Can you give it to them? Then do not be too eager to deal out death in judgment. For even the very wise cannot see all ends.—Gandalf, *The Fellowship of the Ring* (in reference to Bilbo's mercy to Gollum)

> The wise speak only of what they know.—*The Two Towers*

> It is not our part to master all the tides of the world, but to do what is in us for the succor of those years wherein we are set, uprooting the evil in the fields that we know, so that those who live after may have clean earth to till. What weather they shall have is not ours to rule.—*The Return of the King*

What does it mean to be wise? I think it is acknowledging that you don't know everything and can't know everything. To be wise means to know you are not.

When we think about King Solomon in the Bible, we remember the king after he received wisdom from God. We see a man who asks God for wisdom, and God grants it to him like it is some kind of superpower. Let's examine exactly how Solomon achieved his wisdom.

71

When Solomon first met God after taking the throne following his father's death, he says:

> And now, O LORD my God, thou hast made thy servant king in place of David my father, although I am but a little child; I do not know how to go out or come in. And thy servant is in the midst of thy people whom thou hast chosen, a great people, that cannot be numbered or counted for multitude. Give thy servant therefore an understanding mind to govern thy people, that I may discern between good and evil; for who is able to govern this thy great people? (1 Kings 3:7–9)

To be wise is to put yourself forever and always in the role of a student—forever learning knowledge and seeking wisdom. To be wise means recognizing you will never achieve the wisdom of God. It means that, like Solomon, you must acknowledge God as your Lord, master, leader, and teacher. Your will must always be in second place because God's will and knowledge must always be first.

PRAYER

Let's pray the Serenity Prayer together today.

> God grant me the serenity to accept the things I cannot change; courage to change the things I can; and wisdom to know the difference.

MEMORY VERSE

> Trust in the LORD with all your heart, and do not rely on your own insight. In all your ways acknowledge him, and he will make straight your paths. (Proverbs 3:5–6)

OBJECTIVES

1. Discover how Solomon became wise.
2. Read wise proverbs from King Solomon.
3. Practice keeping straight paths.

ACTIVITIES

STRAIGHT PATHS

Prepare: Plan a route where you can play a safe game of follow-the-leader where you will cause the least amount of distraction to others.

Explain: Let's practice keeping our ways straight. Remind the children to be quiet in the hallways in respect of the other classes. Demonstrate how to turn a corner at a ninety-degree angle. Then make lots of turns. Play until you are bored or are losing the attention of your group.

Tip: To help children visualize a ninety-degree angle, show them a carpenter's T square. As an alternative, take two rulers and place them at ninety-degree angles.

Look It Up: How Did Solomon Become Wise?

Prepare: Write 1 Kings 3:5–13 on a whiteboard, piece of paper, or flip chart where all the children can see it.

Explain: People say Solomon is responsible for writing the last three books of this section: Proverbs, Ecclesiastes, and Song of Solomon. He was known as a very wise king. As a result, he was also a very wealthy king. This story is about how Solomon became wise.

> Ask: Was Solomon awake when God was talking to him? What did God say to Solomon? What did Solomon ask for? Why did he ask for wisdom? If you were Solomon, what would you have asked for? What did God think of his answer? What else did God give Solomon?

Look It Up: Solomon's Sayings

Prepare: On a piece of paper, draw a thought bubble, a quote bubble, and a heart. In the quote bubble write the word "Proverbs," in the thought bubble write the word "Ecclesiastes," and in the heart write "Song of Solomon." On a whiteboard or piece of paper, write Ecclesiastes 3:1–8.

Explain: People believe Solomon was responsible for many of the things that were written in Proverbs, Ecclesiastes, and the Song of Solomon. Proverbs contains things Solomon said. They are wise sayings that sound like commandments. The Song of Solomon is a poem celebrating the love between a husband and a wife. Ecclesiastes is full of things Solomon learned throughout his life. One famous passage in Ecclesiastes was made into a very popular folk rock song.

Read the passage together. As you talk about each of the three books, place the proper quote bubble, thought bubble, or heart by King Solomon's star on the star wall.

Ask: Who has heard this before? What does Solomon mean? Does anything in these verses surprise you? How many books in the Bible did Solomon write? Do you think Solomon was wise? Why or why not?

Hint: If you have time, Proverbs is also accessible to children and fun to read. Explore the book and find some you think the children will like. Some suggestions are: Proverbs 10:1, 4, 12 and Proverbs 11:11.

Tip: Play a YouTube video of Pete Seeger's song, "Turn! Turn! Turn." The original single was sung by a group called The Byrds in 1965. It has since been performed by a number of other musical artists.

Play Solomon Says

Prepare: Find a large space where the children can spread out and play this game without bumping into one another.

Explain: This is a version of Simon Says. Instead of when you hear, "Simon says," only do the actions when the leader says, "Solomon says."

Tips: The quicker you fire out the orders, the more fun this game is. Start slow and then build up to rapid-fire commands. Some fun options: Touch your nose, ear, shoulder, knee, foot, pinky, elbow, hair, shoe, and mouth. Stand up, sit down, lay on the floor, turn around, jump up, squat, march, hop, hop on one leg, and hop on both legs. Nod, close your eyes, raise your right hand, raise your left hand, raise both hands, wave to the front, wave to the rear, wave to the right, and wave to the left.

Prayer/Closing

Prepare: Place the memory verse where the children can easily see it.

Explain: Some people think that when you are wise, you listen more than you speak. Instead of saying our prayer out loud, sit and read it silently for thirty seconds.

Pray: Read the memory verse together silently. See if the children can sit completely silent for thirty seconds. You may have to try a couple of times.

Parent Connection

Take the Memory Verse Home

Encourage the children to pledge to walk straight for a designated amount of time (five minutes, one hour, in the morning, all day, etc.). Explain that walking straight means no curving corners. Demonstrate, again, what it means to walk around corners using only straight lines (a ninty-degree turn).

Future Books

A Promise Fulfilled

This book gives a detailed view of the history of the Israelite people through the eyes of the major and minor prophets and culminates in a study of the Gospels and Jesus's birth, ministry, death, and resurrection. In this book, we not only solve the mystery behind the tribe of Judah's importance but also discuss the new arrangement God created with his people by literally tearing down the curtain of separation between us and his holy presence. We also explore the next step in writing technology by learning about the creation of papyrus and parchment.

The Birth of the Church

In this study of Acts, Paul's letters, the Epistles, and Revelation, we celebrate Pentecost and then trace the steps of the disciples and Paul as they spread the Good News of Jesus Christ to the secular world. The attention of this series turns from *who* to *where*, as we explore the sites, tastes, and topographies of the countries surrounding the Mediterranean Sea with Paul. Experience harrowing sea adventures, skirmishes, prison breaks, and other hazards of ancient maritime travel. Finally, discover how the Bible has arrived in the form and translations we see today.

Appendix A

Bible Games

Contained on these pages are interactive games to play, no matter what lesson you are doing. Preparation for these games is minimal. Use them to help the children memorize the books of the Bible.

Can You Say It?

Here is a game to help students learn to pronounce difficult Bible book names.

Prepare: Find a large, bouncy ball. Soft, gymnasium-style balls used for playing foursquare are better than harder ones such as basketballs.

How to Play:

1. Have participants stand in a circle. One person holds the ball.
2. The person with the ball bounces it to another person in the circle while saying the name of a book of the Bible (i.e., "Genesis"). The second person catches the ball and bounces it to a third person while saying the same book name. Continue until everyone in the circle has had the ball and has had a chance to say the name of the book.
3. Repeat the game with the remaining book names in the lesson.

Can You Remember It?

Here is a game to help children remember the books of the Bible in order.

Prepare: Find a large, bouncy ball. Soft, gymnasium-style balls used to play foursquare are better than harder ones such as basketballs.

How to Play:

1. Have participants stand in a circle. One person holds the ball.
2. The person with the ball bounces it to someone else while saying a book of the Bible. The second person catches the ball and bounces it to a third person while saying the next book of the Bible in order, and so on.

3. If someone says an incorrect book, start over with the book you began with. Continue until all the books are said in the correct order.
4. Repeat until bored.

Add It!

This is a game to help children remember the books of the Bible in order.

1. With the children sitting or standing in a circle, have one child start by saying the first book of the Bible.
2. The next child in the circle says the first two books of the Bible.
3. The next child in the circle says the first three books of the Bible. Keep going until all the books you are practicing have been said.
4. Repeat until bored.

Bible Book Race (Quiet Version)

This game helps children, who are being too rowdy, to focus.

Prepare: Find or create several sets of Bible flash cards or Bible books.

How to Play:

1. Using the Bible book flash cards or the Bible books you have created, race to see how fast the children can put all the books or a section of the books in order.
2. The first few times, let them use the front of their Bibles as a cheat sheet. Amp up the competition by having them put the books in order by memory.
3. This game can be played in teams or individually.

Bible Book Race (Rowdy Version)

This is a game to help children expend pent up energy.

Prepare: Find or create several sets of Bible flash cards or Bible books.

How to Play:

1. Using the Bible book flash cards or the Bible books you have created, race to see how fast the children can put a section of the books in order. For this game to work properly, you narrow your selection of books to only one book per child. For example, if you have five children in your classroom, choose a section of five consecutive books to put in order.
2. Place the cards or books you have chosen in a pile at one end of the room.
3. Line the children up at the opposite end of the room.

4. When you say "Go," have the children race to grab only one card or book each.

5. When they have grabbed their book or card, have them line up so their books are in the correct order.

6. The first few times, let them use the fronts of their Bibles as a cheat sheet. Amp up the competition by having them put the books in order by memory.

Which Book is Missing? (Quiet)

This is a version of a whodunit guessing game and is fun to play.

Prepare: Find or create several sets of Bible flash cards or Bible books.

How to Play:

1. Using the Bible flash cards or Bible books you have created, put the section of the Bible you are memorizing on a table. Have the children start by putting the books in the correct order.

2. Choose one child to be *it*. When in doubt, a good rule is to let the youngest go first.

3. While the child who is it closes his or her eyes or leaves the room, the other children pick one to three books out of the group, remove them from the table, and hide them.

4. The child who is it, opens his or her eyes or comes back into the room and must guess which of the books is missing.

5. Repeat until everyone who wants a chance to be *it* has had one.

Balloon Pop (Rowdy)

Here is another game to expend pent up energy!

Prepare: Purchase enough balloons so there is one balloon for each book of the Bible you are studying. You will also need a piece of paper, a pen, and scissors. Write the names of the Bible books you are learning on a small piece of paper and insert the paper into a balloon. Blow up the balloons, tie them, and place them all over the room.

How to Play:

1. Tell the children that the names of the books of the Bible are hidden inside of the balloons. As fast as they can, they are to find a balloon, pop it by sitting on it, and find the name inside it.

2. Once the balloons are popped, they are to place the book names in order on a table.

3. Make it a race against the clock. Tell the children you will time them to see how fast they can go.

Appendix B
Classroom Resources

The following list of resources has helped me in developing this curriculum series. Use some or all of them to enhance your lessons and to help you and the children you serve learn more about the Bible.

What the Bible is All About: Bible Handbook for Kids by Dr. Henrietta Mears (Ventura, California: Gospel Light Publishing, 1986). This is a visually stimulating book, which contains background information on the books of the Bible and reinforces the overarching message about God and his plan of salvation found within the Bible's pages.

The One-Stop Bible Atlas by Nick Page (Oxford, England: Lion Hudson, 2010). This is my go-to book for all kinds of helpful maps and diagrams. Buy it. It is worth adding to your library just for the information it contains.

Rose Book of Bible Charts, Maps, and Time Lines by Rose Publishing (Torrance, California, 2005). Here is another very nice book of charts and diagrams that are interesting and informative.

Rose Guide to the Temple by Dr. J. Randall Price (Torrance, California: Rose Publishing, 2012). This book is an excellent reference with fun drawings and cutaways of the Tabernacle, Solomon's Temple, the rebuilt Temple, and Herod's Temple.

Then and Now Bible Maps by Rose Publishing (Torrance, California, 2005). This book has the same maps that are in the back of your Bible but with plastic overlays that give you the lines and names of the area today. This book is very helpful in making the connection that the Bible is a book about real places and people.

For help with word pronunciations from the Bible, go to: http://www.thebibleworkshop.com/bible-name-pronunciation/

It is a great place to play an audio clip of hard-to-pronounce Bible names and places and to ensure you are saying them correctly.

STAR TEMPLATE

Star Wall (sample)

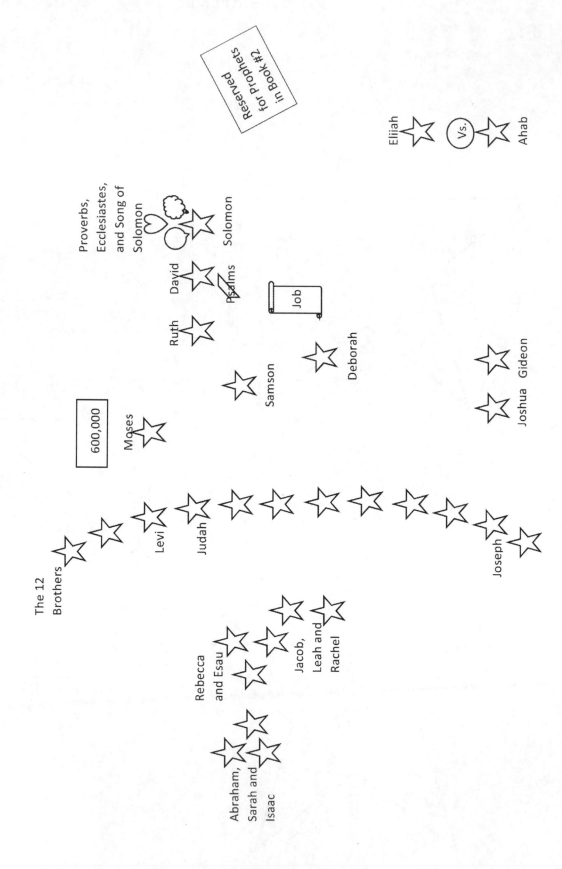

ABOUT THE AUTHOR

In 2012, Brenda Hicks was asked to take over teaching her church's third grade Sunday School class. Third grade is the year the children of her church receive their first "real" Bibles. She gladly accepted the challenge and spent the next four years writing a curriculum that would teach children the wonders of the books of the Bible. Brenda holds a Bachelor of Arts degree from Kansas State University in English with a Creative Writing emphasis and a Master of Arts Degree from Wichita State University. She is also a graduate of all four years of Disciple Bible Study. Prior to writing this curriculum, she created a bible based preschool curriculum with her sister-in-law, a Kindergarten teacher, which was purchased and utilized in several  Kansas churches and daycare facilities. Brenda lives with her husband and two sons in Winfield, Kansas where she works as the Director of Financial Aid at Southwestern College.

Printed in the United States
By Bookmasters